A CRUEL NECESSITY

Hambleden and the Civil War

Chris Whitehead

The cover image is from 'Cromwell Gazing at the Body of Charles I' by Paul Delaroche 1831 (Musée des Beaux-Arts, Nimes). On viewing the body, he was said to have muttered 'A cruel necessity'. Curiously, he seems to be attired as a cavalier.

Birch Cottage Publications
Pheasants Hill
Hambleden
RG9 6SN

Email: chriswhiteheadhambleden@gmail.com

© 2023 This publication is in copyright. No reproduction of any part may take place without the written permission of the author

ISBN 978-1-915787-63-7

Produced by Biddles Books Limited,
King's Lynn, Norfolk

When the Head warred against the Members & the Member against the Head, When Protestants against Protestants, brothers against brothers, sons against fathers and fathers against sons, sought the destruction of one another, then was this great Creature neare the slaughter of it selfe. All were wearied out with Civill warre, with the plundering of houses and the depopulating of Townes.

Sir Bulstrode Whitelocke.

An extract from the John Rocque's map of 1761 –
probably the oldest detailed map of the area

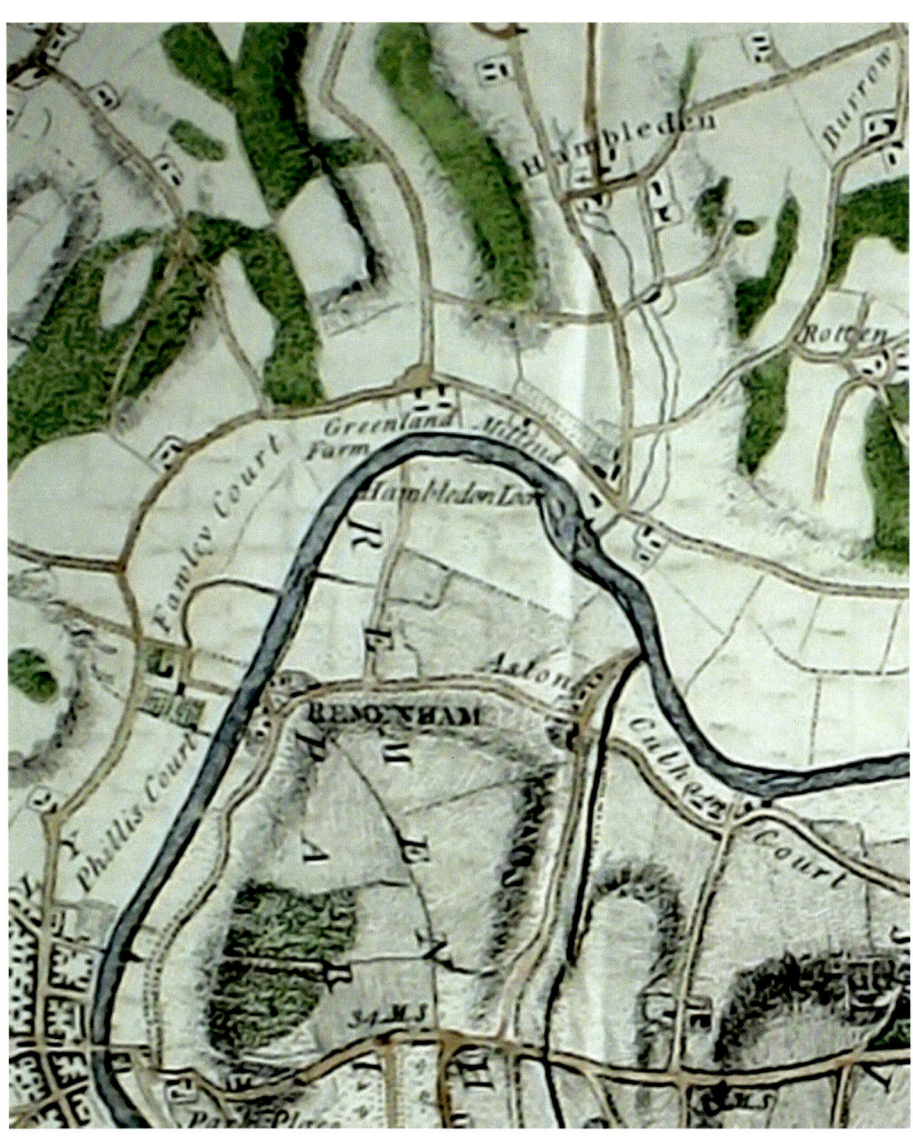

Contents

Introduction		1
Chapter 1:	Hambleden	5
Chapter 2:	King and Country	11
Chapter 3:	Fawley Court	21
Chapter 4:	Greenlands	27
Chapter 5:	Henley and Phyllis Court	39
Chapter 6:	Afterwards	49
Postscript		57

Appendixes

1. Timeline — 59
2. Dramatis Personae — 61
3. Cormorants and Lovebirds — 63

Introduction

The history of the Civil War (1642-1651)[1] is now mostly forgotten, so that much of the horror, suffering, bitterness and strength of feeling about the issues have faded into the background. Today only a vague impression of such an important but horrific episode in our history remains. There are surprisingly few physical remains to remind modern generations about the war, nor are there any graves or memorabilia of the soldiers that fell. At the site of the battle of Naseby, where thousands died, a busy road tears by. At Edgehill, a nearby pub garden houses a modest panel sketchily explaining what happened. Only Marston Moor has a nineteenth century monumental pillar and a few plastic signs. Is there a reluctance to acknowledge a difficult and traumatic period in our past, a dread of reigniting religious hatred? Locally, there is nothing to remind us of the actions that took place at the three Thames-side Manor houses of Greenlands, Fawley Court and Phyllis Court, nor of the military activity in Henley. There is a plaque on the wall of Hambleden Manor House telling us that Lord Cardigan of Light Brigade infamy once lived there – but nothing to let us know that King Charles I had spent a night there while fleeing from Oxford. I leave it up you to decide which of these two events has the more historical significance.

It's as though he whole sad affair has been airbrushed from our history, that England has turned its back on its most influential war – the conflict that

---

1 What I refer to as 'The Civil War' was, in fact, a series of three Civil Wars and political machinations between Parliamentarians and Royalists, mainly over the manner of England's governance and issues of religious freedom. The first (1642–1646) and second (1648–1649) wars pitted the supporters of King Charles I against the supporters of the Long Parliament, while the third (1649–1651) saw fighting between supporters of King Charles II and supporters of the Rump Parliament. The wars also involved the Scottish Covenanters and Irish Confederates. The wars ended with Parliamentarian victory over the Scots at the Battle of Worcester on 3 September 1651

resulted in the abolition of the Monarchy and the House of Lords to be replaced by a republic and military rule. It planted the roots of the supremacy of Parliament over the Monarchy that we are so familiar with today and ended the monopoly of the Church of England on Christian worship.

Ask anyone about it and they will doubtless tell you of romantic cavaliers and devout roundheads, and the execution of the King. Civil War re-enactment societies featuring merry cavaliers in plumed hats and long-faced roundheads in round helmets bear as little relevance to reality as cowboys and Indians in an old Western. How could their re-enactments, however blood curdling, reflect the awful violence of the war and the terror felt by those involved in it, either as participants or civilians? It is easy to forget (if we ever knew) that the Civil War was the most lethal conflict England had suffered since the Conquest. Around 86,000 were killed in combat, while another 129,000 civilians succumbed to the diseases that accompanied war. Infant mortality reached the highest level ever recorded. These losses in a population of 4-5 million are proportionately much higher than those Britain suffered in the Great War.

The purpose of these few pages is not to dig into the labyrinthine politics of the early seventeenth century, nor to examine the tactics of the major battles. It's aims are much more modest – to describe the sieges and skirmishes along the River Thames between Greenlands and Henley, and the impact of these relatively minor incidents on the people of Hambleden. Minor perhaps in the scale of things, but not minor to those involved. In doing so, I have relied on the diaries of Sir Bulstrode Whitelocke and of Sir Samuel Luke, Scoutmaster (spymaster) to the Earl of Essex, Captain-General and Chief Commander of the Parliamentarian army. Whitelocke was the leading personage in the district. He was the owner of Fawley Court and Phyllis Court as well as several properties in Henley. As a moderate parliamentarian (described by his biographer Ruth Spalding as an 'improbable puritan'), he was MP for Great Marlow in the Long Parliament of 1640-1648, in which he was Lord Keeper of the Great Seal of England (now the Lord Chancellor). His rather unusual Christian name came about when his uncle Edmund Whitelocke, being one of his godfathers, announced at his Christening that the child was to be called Bulstrode. The vicar demurred, but

Edmund insisted that he bear his mother's name, "Bulstrode or Elizabeth, let them choose which they please"

Where possible I have reproduced their diaries as they were written, with their original quirky punctuation and spellings[2]. They are worth persevering with as through them I hope you may be able to capture a flavour of the age. Whitelocke's diaries are especially peculiar in that they are written in third person.

Several people have helped me in preparing these notes, and I thank them all. In particular, I have received special help from Professor Adrian Bell of Reading University who filled in many gaps on the siege of Greenlands. I am also most grateful to the Henley Society for their permission to quote from their essay on 'Henley and the Civil War' by Ann Cottingham. Janet Smith of the Marlow Society also provided useful insights. Charles Hussey and my wife, Jo, masterful editors both, made many valuable comments. Gray Joliffe and I designed the cover over much wine.

---

2 Which play havoc with Spellcheck!

Chapter 1

Hambleden

For the first forty years of the seventeenth century, Hambleden was the same idyllic place it is today. The Hambleden Valley, sitting between Henley-on-Thames and Marlow, is bordered by the river Thames to the south and, to the north, east and west, by gentle lower valley slopes which become steeper in the upper reaches. It seems to have a sort of quiet sensuality being generally moist, lush and soft, with ample curves, a temperate climate and unthreatening wildlife. The valley contains an intricate mixture of hamlets, medieval farms in hollows in the hills, great barns, ancient trees, cavernous holloways and many footpaths, irregularly shaped groves and thick hedges. Woodland, much of which is ancient, crowns the valley tops, creating a physical and visual boundary to the Valley. There is almost a feeling of secrecy about it, and yet its interface with the river Thames at the bottom of the Valley has meant it has never been out of touch with current events. The history of the village has, to a large extent, been a function of its geographical position on the river. The Thames has been both a highway and a natural boundary forever. This may be of little importance today, but in Stuart England it put Hambleden in the centre of the ebb and flow of political and commercial life.

A Cruel Necessity – Hambleden and the Civil War

It was, of course, a lot smaller four hundred years ago, but did at least boast a brand-new manor house[3] (called the New House) built in 1604 to replace the old timber and wattle house that was on the site of where Kenricks stands today.

It was one of the grandest houses in the area with fine glass windows, and was unusual in as much as it was built in the centre of the village. At the same time the homes of better off people like yeoman farmers were being enlarged and having new features incorporated such as a separate kitchen (instead of the open hall), proper upper chambers reached by a staircase (instead of a mere loft with a ladder), permanent wooden panelling (wainscoting) and glass in the windows. Rush covered floors were replaced by matting or carpets. The precincts included a walled kitchen garden and flower gardens – then becoming the fashion. Burrow Farm is a good example of this. Following the example of the Manor House, it too is built of brick and flint. Their construction was seen as a vote of confidence, not only in the future of the village, but in that of England as a whole.

The New House was built by the then Lord of the Manor, Emanuel Scrope, 1st Earl of Sunderland, 11th Baron Scrope of Bolton. AH Stanton describes him as an 'unfavourable' character[4], so no one was too confounded that on his death in 1630 he left his estates not to his legitimate relatives, but to his illegitimate children. After that date, the estate was split up. The estate, but not the New House, passed into the hands of Emanuel's second illegitimate daughter and her husband Thomas Savage, 3rd Earl Rivers. Emanuel's widow, Elizabeth, Dowager Countess of Sunderland, remained in the House after his death as part of her marriage settlement. She died in 1654.[5]

---

3 This image shows how central the house is. The extension on the left is, of course, modern.
4 'On Chiltern Slopes' p21
5 Shades of the sale of Hambleden Estate in 2007.

Chapter 1: Hambleden

Hambleden was a farming community, as it had been for hundreds of years. Grazing of sheep and cattle on the often-boggy valley bottom gave way to woodland and waste on the valley sides, which afforded rough grazing as well as fuel. On top of the surrounding hills were very large fields, each divided into an apparently haphazard patchwork of interlocking furlongs served by a maze of tracks and fieldways, enabling villagers to reach their scattered strips of land for cultivation. The whole effect was to create a countryside round Hambleden that had a markedly different appearance from today in that it was much more open; there were very few fences and hedges. Around the village were a collection of 'closes', rather like modern allotments, allowing individual farmers to keep a pig and grow vegetables. Although the ancient practice of strip farming was still prevalent, the power of the manor was significantly weaker than in feudal times, and little was owed to the Manor as of right. Farmers were free to take any surplus produce to the Thursday market in Henley.

Most grain was taken to Hambleden Mill where it was converted to flour. The village bakery continued to bake fine bread. In addition to the baker there was a butcher and no doubt a candlestick maker, and, of course, a blacksmith[6]. A well in the village square supplied water. In short, the village was more or less self-sufficient. Anything that was not available locally would be obtained at the Henley market or bought from an itinerant tinker.

Life revolved around the Church, both physically and spiritually. The English Church, the least Protestant of all the European reformed churches, was by the standards of the day, fairly tolerant and intellectually diverse. No one was burned for heresy during Charles' reign, and the execution of witches was discouraged and was in steep decline[7]. Traditional games were permitted after Church on Sundays, such as dancing, archery, leaping and vaulting. In a country in which the Church was the crucible for all cultural and personal lives, in which unbelief was unthinkable, religion had an inescapable social and political impact that

---

[6] HJ Massingham in 'Chiltern Country' tells us that the parish register of 1640 inscribed ten yeomen, a bargeman, a glover, a weaver, a bricklayer, a carpenter, a lath-shaver, a wharfinger, a miller, a 'mayson', a smith, a wheelwright, a flour-maker, a hemp-dresser, a shoemaker and a joiner.

[7] It later revived sharply under the Puritans.

is now lost in England and Wales[8]. The most and least religious Britons shared the same moral universe. Concepts such as grace, sin, heaven and hell were reference points for a religiously inflected common sense.

There was, however, an undercurrent of discontent. Some suspected that the King was leading the Church back to a more Roman Catholic doctrine. They believed that the Church needed to become more Protestant, and should be 'purified' of all Catholic practice. Through Puritan endeavour there ran an evangelical instinct: the zeal to promote, by preaching and reading, the Gospel truths which bring salvation. Puritans were repelled by the obstacles to that advance: by worldly vanities and sensual delights which distract or destroy the soul, and by display and ceremony in worship which substitute images for the word of God and idolatry for faith.

Anglicans maintained that the persuasive power of the Church lay not in sermons, on which Puritans laid too much stress, but in the comely observation of the sacraments in set forms of prayer and worship, and in the affirmations and solaces and verbal rhythms of the Prayer Book, which placed the rituals of birth, marriage and death in the great and essentially unaltering continuum of time. Where Puritans tended to think of church buildings as mere venues, the plainer the better[9], for the gathering of believers, and frequently took little care of their upkeep, Anglicans set store by their appearance to the outward eye.

In short, to Puritans, the Reformation had not gone far enough; to Anglicans it had gone, or threatened to go, too far.

This was a quandary that had faced all rulers after Henry VIII introduced the ecclesiastical element into the political. It was one Charles struggled to overcome. His instinct was with the Anglicans; he tended to equate Puritanism with sedition. The situation reached its critical zenith during his reign, resulting in a fragmentation of Parliament and the creation of rival factions acting in

---

8 The 2021 Census revealed that England and Wales are now minority Christian countries for the first time since census data collection began, and arguably for the first time in fifteen centuries, with less than half the population describing themselves as Christian, and a big increase in the proportion of people saying they have no religion.

9 For example, the United Reformed Church at Pheasants Hill. Though built much later (1807), it has a plainness of which Puritans would have been proud two hundred years earlier.

concert not only against themselves but eventually against Charles. England was in religious turmoil, with two alternative versions of the Protestant faith at loggerheads.

Although most villagers in Hambleden were content to leave their spiritual lives in the hands of their rector, John Domelaw, memories of the Gunpowder Plot still lingered. In truth, in a conservative society, very few wanted things to change. The Church was important, but not as much as the weather. Nevertheless, there was enough grumbling for a few malcontents to begin to stir things up by circulating pamphlets and delivering 'tree stump' sermons.

It wasn't as if the so-called Puritans were pushing at an open door. England was enjoying unparalleled political and social peace, and continued to do so until shortly before the outbreak of the war. England was a country that respected authority in the form of king and parliament and accepted the need for ordered government, functioning according to known rules. Violent religious persecution had been replaced by tacit toleration of diversity. While there was undoubtedly political and religious discord, there was no prospect of revolt, no discernible way by which the adversaries could have crossed the unthinkable gulf into Civil War much less execute the King.

So, in 1640, it came as a bit of a surprise when word filtered though that the Scots, angered by the King's religious changes and interference, had invaded England as far south as Newcastle. This came as a huge shock to the citizens of England; there had been no large-scale Scottish incursion since 1543. Indeed, violence in general had greatly declined; the country was experiencing a period of social tranquillity not to be seen again until the nineteenth century. It was a demilitarised and peaceful country by the standards of the time, or indeed by those of our own day. Few people owned weapons, so Bulstrode Whitelocke of Fawley Court must have recorded the following with some concern....

> ....*The warre with the Scots being begun Whitelocke, as others did, furnished himself with a barrell of Gunpowder, & Bulletts & 20 Carabines, with swords & necessary provisions, & hung them up in his Hall, men differed much in opinion touching the warre most wishing it had not been begun.*

From then on Whitelocke noted that the speed and severity of the crisis had an air of unreality. He identified a clear chain of causation between the proliferation of printed attacks and the outbreak of musket fire, commenting....

> ....*It is strange to note how we have insensible slid into the beginning of a Civil War, by one unexpected accident after another, as waves of the sea, which have brought us thus far; and we scarce know how, but from paper combats, by declarations, remonstrances, protestations, votes, messages, answers and replies, we are now come to the question of raising forces, and naming a general and officers of an army*

Writing to his wife in the summer of 1642, he ruminated about what the impending Civil War would be like....

> ....*We must surrender up all our laws, liberties, properties and living into the hands of insolent mercenaries, whose rage and violence will command us.*

He predicted that amongst the first casualties would be *reason honour and justice*. The world that he and his wife loved in the peacefulness of Fawley Court would be turned upside down, with base folk lording it over the noble, the profane usurping the pious.

No one really thought war would come about. Rather like the slide into the Great War, the country seemed to sleepwalk, absent-mindedly, into it. Only a small minority of activists were genuinely committed to one or other of the causes. Undoubtedly the great majority of local people hoped that war could be avoided and life would continue as normal. Even if it could not, they hoped they would be able to stay out of it. In any case, they believed one good battle would end it. But, sadly, one good battle did not end it; the village was drawn willy-nilly into the war, which the villagers faced with their usual dogged cussedness.

Life in Hambleden would not continue as normal.

Chapter 2

King and Country

If you were attempting to devise the worst possible system of government for a country, you would be hard pressed to come up with anything more absurd than the Tudor and Stuart's idea of an hereditary monarchy. The concept is appealing only in its simplicity; one man[10] is in charge of everything - the government, the economy, and the Church. The best man to nurture the nation's religious well-being is apparently also the best man to lead the army into battle. He is the legislature, the executive and the judiciary all rolled into one. The man's qualification for the post is simply the fact that his father had done it. He then rules for his entire life irrespective of how well he performs until the job passes to his eldest son, whatever his suitability for the position. At best you would be concerned at the random quality of men that this system threw up. But of course, it is worse than that, because the formula is almost guaranteed to create arrogant, blinkered and over protected individuals who have never been criticised, corrected or had to consider the possibility that they might not know best. In this sense the heir to the throne was possibly the very worst person in the entire country to become ruler.

Charles I ascended the throne in 1625 with a combination of all the arrogance and certainty of the English upper classes. He was only five feet four (1.63m) even with his head. He stammered, and fatally set about offending a significant proportion of his subjects. While to those close to him he could be charming and considerate, to others he was seen as being dazzlingly short(!) of endearing qualities. While far from being a stupid man, Charles was temperamentally

---

10 The monarch could, of course, have been a queen as in Queen Elizabeth I, but for the sake of simplicity I have stuck with the male gender.

authoritarian, holding to an exalted notion of the nature of kingship as God-given and denying opposition any legitimacy. Cold and aloof, he lacked basic political skills and judgment and came increasingly to be seen as untrustworthy. He made concessions with the greatest of reluctance, and sought to reverse them later, and gained a well-deserved reputation for deviousness by negotiating with opponents while, at the same time, planning to use force against them. He pursued unpopular policies, none more so than his disastrous religious policy, and he was personally responsible for the decision to impose the English prayer book on the Scots which set in motion the whole chain of events that would eventually lead to civil war. Yet the responsibility for the conflict cannot be laid entirely at Charles' door even though he had an important part to play in making it possible.[11]

He had to face three fundamental problems, problems that would have taxed any ruler – the Church, the fiscal system and the diverse kingdoms of the state, the first two of which were inherited from Queen Elizabeth.

We have already discussed the problems of the Church – how it was being pulled in two directions, while most people were happy to stay in the middle. Meanwhile, the ancient fiscal system failed to provide the Crown with the increasing costs of governing, and especially of fighting. Modern war with artillery, fortresses, larger armies and bigger warships was expensive. To raise the necessary funds, Charles needed to go to Parliament. But Charles believed in the Divine Right of Kings. This was the belief that he had been put in charge of the country by God, so therefore did not need permission from Parliament in order to make decisions. He famously argued…*Princes are not bound to give an account of their Actions but to God alone.*

Consequently, in 1629, he decided to dissolve Parliament and rule without it. When the King ordered the Commons to adjourn, members held the Speaker down in his chair and locked the door to keep the royal messenger out. This

---

[11] A recent biography of Charles by Mark Kishlansky makes a case for his defence, arguing that the accepted view of Charles and his reign has been utterly distorted: the narratives spun by the parliamentarian propaganda of the 1640s have only grown stronger in the intervening centuries, so that we now vacillate between viewing Charles as an idiot at best and a tyrant at worst. What began as propaganda, says Kishlansky, has been transmuted into seeming fact.

drama is decorously re-enacted at each State Opening, when the royal messenger, Black Rod, has the door of the Commons slammed in his face, and is made to knock on it for admittance. Parliament did not sit again until 1640.

There was much resentment against the quasi-feudal means that Charles employed to raise revenue. Thus, the gentry found some common cause with those of lower social status. In Skirmett, a Mr Robert Shepwash of Goddards refused to contribute and was hauled up before a committee of the Privy Council at Beaconsfield.

The third problem was how to govern three Kingdoms (England, Scotland and Ireland) whose historic enmities were now aggravated by a widening religious gulf. The Scots wanted to be more Presbyterian and the Irish more Catholic. No one knew how to reconcile these differences. The only solution seemed to rest on the military option. A perfect storm! Knowing that Charles was in desperate need of money to fight Scotland after their invasion, Parliament, now recalled, placed heavy demands on him in return for their support. Charles refused to agree to these demands and the relationship between the House of Commons and the King became increasingly fraught, though even up to this point the conventions of deference still persuaded MPs to attribute misrule to evil advisors and conspirators around the monarch. Most parliamentarians in 1642 were not supporters of a party that was intent on wresting power from the king and vesting it in parliament. They still hoped for an eventual political settlement that would combine all the essential features of the ancient constitution, including a critical role for the monarchy but with a more decisive role for Parliament.

As well as the vast majority of the two Houses of Parliament, the great bulk of the governing classes - the nobility and gentry, government officers, lawyers, mayors and aldermen of the towns, and the leading merchants deplored the thought of resolving the disagreement by force, and still hoped for and expected agreement between the king, Lords and Commons

Charles grew more and more frustrated, until, on January 4, 1642, he decided to go to the House of Commons himself to apprehend the five men who he considered to be the Parliamentarian ringleaders. Accompanied by about 400 armed men, he entered the Commons chamber to the amazement of all therein. Addressing Speaker Lenthall[12], he said *Mr Speaker, I must for a time make bold with your chair.* Lenthall vacated it. Calling first for one of the members, and then another, Charles was met with total silence[13]. He asked the speaker where they were. Kneeling, Lenthall responded with extraordinary courage….

> ….*May it please your majesty, I have neither eyes to see nor tongue to speak in this place but as this House is pleased to direct me whose servant I am here; and I humbly beg your majesty's pardon that I cannot give any other answer than this to what your majesty is pleased to demand of me.*

It was the first time that a Speaker had declared his allegiance to the liberty of parliament rather than the will of the monarch. However, the five MPs had been forewarned and had slipped away by water into the city, so Charles failed to make any arrests while totally alienating both chambers[14]. After this rebuff the King left London on January 10 for the north of England. He raised his standard at Nottingham in August, eventually establishing his court and military headquarters in Christ Church College, Oxford.

---

12 William Lenthall was born in Hart Street, Henley-on-Thames. The house, now called Speaker's House, in which he was born still stands (see above)
13 Whitelocke considered himself fortunate to have absented himself from the House on the fateful day.
14 Because of Charles's actions, to this day the monarch is still not allowed into the House of Commons.

Chapter 2: King and Country

Oxford would remain his base until late April 1646 when he slipped out of the city as it became encircled by Parliamentarian troops He was disguised as a groom to his companion, Lord Ashburnham, and was accompanied by his personal priest. They rode towards Henley, a town the King knew well. He is reported to have visited the Red Lion in 1632 and again in 1642 after the battle of Edgehill enroute to Oxford, accompanied by Price Rupert and his dog, Boy[15]. His painted Royal Coat of Arms is preserved over the fireplace in one of the guestrooms. [16]

In 1646 Henley was in the hands of the Parliamentarians, so they turned off the main route at Lower Assendon where they took refuge in a barn[17]. The next morning, they moved on, up the hill towards Fawley where they rested under an ancient oak, still extant, and now called Charles' Staghead. This veteran tree[18], with a girth of 7.30 metres and a stag head form, can be seen easily from the bridleway of the Oxfordshire Way footpath. It is almost certainly more than 380 years old so would have been standing at the time of the English Civil War. Having watered themselves and their horses, they rode across country, keeping well clear of the Parliamentary strongholds at Fawley Court and Phyllis

---

15 Boy, sometimes called Pudel; a large white hunting poodle, accompanied Rupert everywhere from 1642 until the dog's death at Marston Moor

16 As the Red Lion was in the middle of Henley's dockland in the 1640's, I wonder whether the King would have stayed there. Mixing with the hoi polloi was not his style. It sems to me that the painting of the coat of arms is no real evidence. It is much more probable that he would have stayed in the comfortable Bell Inn at semi-rural Northfield End that Prince Rupert was using as his base in 1642.

17 The farmer is said to have been hanged by Oliver Cromwell's men for harbouring the King.

18 This is the tree taken on April 28 2023, exactly 377 years after Charles rested beneath it.

A Cruel Necessity – Hambleden and the Civil War

Court, to Hambleden Manor where they stayed the night. There were so many spies in the area that is unlikely that their presence went unnoticed. We are led to believe that Whitelocke turned a blind eye. A week later, moving north[19], the King surrendered to a Scottish army at Southwell, Nottinghamshire. He was eventually handed over to the English Parliament by the Scots and imprisoned. Within three years[20] he found himself on a scaffold outside the Banqueting Hall in Whitehall, awaiting the blow of the executioner's axe before a throng of his subjects[21], about to be beheaded *as a tyrant, traitor, murderer, and public enemy to the good people of this nation.*

Where did it all go wrong?

* * * * *

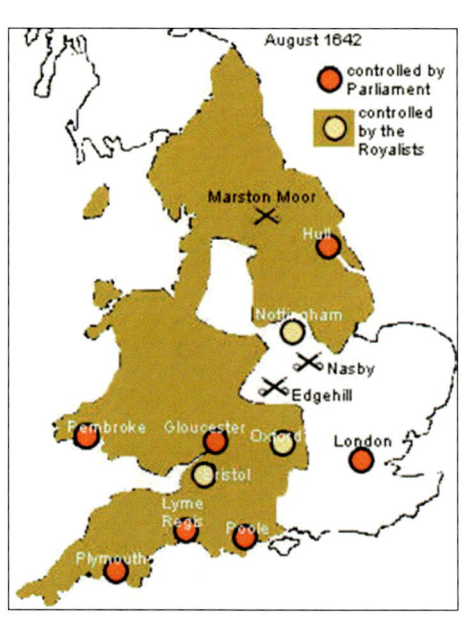

Between August 1642 and January 1649, the country was split down the middle. In England, the populous and prosperous southeast, London and East Anglia were strongest in their support for Parliament. The west, including Wales, was mainly for the King. In general terms the local dividing line was the Buckinghamshire/Oxfordshire border, and the loyalties of the various houses and estates reflects

---

19 It has been suggested that that the place name Rotten Row was derived from the route that the King took on leaving Hambleden : Route du Roi.
20 On 30 January 1649.
21 Detail from 'An Eyewitness Representation of the Execution of King Charles I of England', 1649 by John Weesop. Note the child standing on his father's shoulders for a better view!

Chapter 2: King and Country

this. The twelve or so miles between Greenlands (Royalist) and Reading (Royalist) took in Bockmer[22] (Royalist), Fawley Court, Phyllis Court and Henley, all Parliamentarian. Hambleden, although under the protection of Whitelocke, was Royalist. Hambleden Parish Register records that old Rector Domelaw died in June 1640, and was replaced by Rector George Roberts. AH Stanton tells us that Rector Roberts had an 'unquiet' time owing to the Civil War. He was turned out of the rectory and went to join the King in Oxford from where he was said to have ridden with the Royalist cavalry. Stanton suggests that this may account for the King spending a night at the New House in April 1646.

The civil conflict impacted on all levels of society. Neighbours, families and communities were divided in their loyalties, and every citizen had to take one side or the other. There was no middle ground, no fence sitting.

We may imagine how society could be absolutely divided when we cast our minds back to the Brexit debate of 2016 when the United Kingdom held a referendum as to whether to leave the European Union or to remain a member of it. A largely populist, emotive, and evidence-free (though well organised) Leave campaign, with the inspired slogan 'Take Back Control' surprisingly carried the day. The slogan urged Britons to shake off the constraints of Brussels and become a proud, sovereign nation once more – a nation that, alone, would decide its fate. As in the 1640's, it was an insurrection against the status quo with a promise to upend the established ways of Westminster government; as in the 1640's, conspiracy theories and misinformation abounded. The argument in both cases tapped into people's impatience with authority and a strong sense of neglect. After Brexit, leavers promised, Britain would be the sole master of its destiny, unburdened by the need to consult, or even accommodate, anyone else. Similarly, in the 1640's, the promise was that Parliament, the representatives of the people, would be able to act independently of the King.

The referendum brought into being a binary of identity where none had existed before. The country, and many families, were split almost down the

---

[22] Sir John Borlase's estates at Bockmer were confiscated during the Commonwealth through his excessive zeal as a Royalist. Afterwards he was allowed to buy them back for £2,400. We are led to understand that after the restoration of the monarchy, Charles II visited Bockmer with Nell Gwyn.

middle (52% to 48%) in favour of the UK leaving the EU. It was a 'splendidly Stuart-style constitutional crisis' as the historian Niall Ferguson put it. Every day we heard phrases once confined to academic study on the lips of newsreaders – such as prerogative power, prorogation and parliamentary sovereignty. As such it had several resonances with the Civil War. In particular, none more so than the absolute division of the country. The polarisation assumed there was no middle ground. The moderates on both sides had been routed. Each side was assumed to be the opposite of the other, obscuring similarities, overlaps and shared feelings. And like Brexit, the Civil War was essentially the north and west of England against the rest of the British Isles. As I write this, seven years after the event, the word 'Brexit' is still toxic. Any discussion about it brings politicians out in a rash of division and disloyalty; no one dares to suggest that it may not be resulting in the halcyon future that we were promised.

Both sides gave their opponents derogatory descriptions. Just as those who wanted to remain in the EU in 2016 were labelled 'remoaners', so before the Civil War broke out, partisans of both sides began to apply an insulting nickname to their opponents, little dreaming that the two scornful labels which they had chosen for each other would ring down through the succeeding centuries. To the Parliamentarians, the Royalists were 'Cavaliers' - a term derived from the Spanish word 'Caballeros', meaning armed troopers or horsemen and implying that they were not serious soldiers. To the Royalists, the Parliamentarians were 'Roundheads' - a reference to the shaved heads of the London apprentices who had been so active in demonstrating their support for Parliament during the months before the fighting began. Both terms reveal a lot about what the two sides thought of each other. In Parliamentarian eyes, the typical Royalist was a dissolute gentleman, possessed of a suspiciously foreign air and prone to acts of sudden violence. As far as the Royalists were concerned, the typical Parliamentarian was a 'base mechanic': a low-born, lumpen townsman, inexperienced in judgment and inelegant in appearance. There was perhaps more than a grain of truth in these stereotypes, but it would be wrong to conclude from them that the Civil War was primarily a class war, a punch up between 'toffs' and 'toughs'.

Why people took different sides between 1642 and 1649 is a complex issue, and there were many differing motives. Political, religious and social matters

Chapter 2: King and Country

were widely debated and frequently distorted by propaganda in broadsheets and pamphlets, most of which were partisan and inflammatory, fostering intolerance of alternative opinion and instability in society. Observing a bewildered English populace deluged by printed appeals and counter-appeals, Giustinian, the Venetian ambassador, pitied….

> ….*these unhappy people attacked by the frequent appearance of these numerous documents, so mutually contradictory.*

The considerations were infinitely more varied and subtle than the two-party labels suggest. Rather like the Brexit issues, most people were somewhere in the middle, open to be persuaded by glib rhetoric. Undoubtedly, some men joined the army to defend their religious freedoms and to further their political ambitions. Many religious dissenters joined the anti-royalists. Others had little choice due to bonds that tied them to local lords and gentlefolk; some were simply loyal. Parliament enticed young men into military service by encouraging apprentices to leave their masters and join the army, meanwhile promising to reward both masters and apprentices for their sacrifices. As in the Great War, many ordinary folks, often poor and disadvantaged, were attracted by the regular pay, food and clothing that army life provided, while a few were attracted by the prospect of glamour and adventure. Initial recruitment was slow as when war broke out, in August 1642, England was in the midst of harvest, the fields covered in shocks of corn or standing golden brown ready for the sickle. The first set piece battle, at Edgehill, in October quickly demonstrated that a clear advantage was enjoyed by neither army, in part because neither side could put enough men into the field, and those that did take part were very raw.

Later, recruitment would gather pace, but once the flow of volunteers subsided, arbitrary and sometimes brutal conscription of infantry was commonplace. By the end of 1642 each army could call on between 60,000 and 70,000 men. Popular allegiance was hardly constant; mutiny, desertion, and transfers of loyalty to victors or captors were common. Training on second rate weapons was desultory – the Royalist pikemen at Edgehill were said to lack armour, and the musketeers lacked swords. Several hundred of them lacked any sort of weapon apart from clubs or improvised polearms. Unsurprisingly, the turnover among the population of soldiery was high.

Did any of the combatants stop and think that the war would forever alter the relationship between monarch and Parliament leading to the long, slow rise of Parliament as the main instrument of power in the land? I think not. The concept of democracy was still foreign and a long way off; electoral reform did not begin to happen until 1832, and then only marginally. Apart from a few zealots, I suspect most people just wanted the whole awful thing to be over, so that they could get on with their lives.

Chapter 3

Fawley Court

Some six months before Charles raised his standard at Nottingham, military activity was seen in the Hambleden valley. In February 1642, Sir Samuel Luke, Spymaster for the Earl of Essex[23], received reports that at….

> ….*Stirmouth*[24] *neere Stoken Church*[25], *Cavallyers being 60 in number were, and took only diet, hay and provender for themselves and their horses, and soe went againe to Oxford saying that they were Parliament soldiers.*

A bewildered Whitelocke recorded that….

> ….*The times began to appear very dreadfull, and all discourses were of the threatening Civil Warre, against which Whitelocke used his best endeavours with many others, butt to no effect.*

Fearing the worst, Whitelocke took defensive measures at Fawley Court and almost killed himself in the process….

---

23 Captain-General and Chief Commander of the Parliamentarian army.
24 Skirmett
25 The site of the village, being on the main London to Oxford road, proved a good resting and changing place for horses and was used by both Royalist and Parliamentarian troops. On two occasions (5 December 1642 and 17 June 1643) skirmishes broke out when both sides arrived at the village together. An original drover's road, to the north of the village, is now a bridleway, called Colliers Lane, the current road having been constructed in 1824.

A Cruel Necessity – Hambleden and the Civil War

....*Whitelocke was well furnished with pikes, muskets[26], pistols, powder, bullet, armes and good horses, which were often trayned by his household servants. He escaped there two great daungers, one by a fall from an unruly horse, the other by the blow of a pistol, which brake, & beat out many of his teeth, & loosened the rest, yet by the goodness of God, the bullet & stroke did him no further hurt, only it caused great pain in his teeth, & was a hindrance to his eating & to his speaking.*

In November Luke received reports of....

....*about 1500 horse at Stoken Church, and some at Henley and some at Marlow.*

These were the advance party of the King's army under Prince Rupert as they moved from Oxford towards London in an attempt to retake the capital.

---

26 Muskets were pretty useless. The musket in common use was a heavy matchlock and needed to be supported (as may be seen from this image) which even a trained soldier could not hope to fire more than once a minute. Though it might kill or maim at 200 yards it was not likely to hit the target at a range of more than 50 yards. The reason for this inaccuracy was that the bullet did not fit the smooth-bore barrel at all tightly, and therefore, when propelled towards the target, it tended to wander. The disadvantages of match were all too obvious: by night it could betray the position of the musketeers, and in foul weather it simply went out.

Chapter 3: Fawley Court

Whitelocke's house at Fawley Court was singled out for ill-treatment. In 1642 Whitelocke wrote in his diary that his wife was expecting their seventh child but refused to move from Fawley Court as….

> …. *being very neer her time of childbirth, was the more frighted att the preparations for Warre, butt being of a gallant Spirit and affected to the Parlement, she did the better endure it.*

After the birth, Whitelocke persuaded her to go with him and the two eldest children to London; the remaining five, the oldest of whom was only six and the youngest, the newly born Hester (presumably because a journey to London might prove too arduous or facilities in London deemed inadequate for a newborn), were sent to be looked after by his tenant William Cooke up at Fawley.

Whitelocke takes up the story, providing a graphic description of the damage that the Royalist army did to his beloved family home, one that held so many special memories for him. We can sense the anger in his notes….

> ….*The King resolved to march to London, his Army advanced to Reading, Henley, & those parts, & a Regiment under Sir John Byron*[27] *quartered att Whitelocke's house att Fawley Court, whereof his tenant, William Cooke & his servants having some notice, they threw into the Mote there pewter, brasse, and iron things, & removed some of his tenants' houses, & into the woods, some of his books, linen & household stuff, as much as the short warning would permit, Sir John Byron & his brothers commanded the horse quartered there to commit no insolence, nor to plunder Whitelocke's goods, but 1,000 of them being in & about his house, there was no insolence or outrage which such guests use to commit upon an Ennemy but these brutish common soldiers did att Fawley Court.*
>
> *There they had their whores, they spent & consumed in one night 100 loade of Corne and hey, littered their horses with good wheate sheafes,*

---

27 Samuel Pepys recorded that, after his death in 1652, Byron's widow became the 17th (!!) mistress of Charles II. Surely one for the Guinness Book of Records? The current king has some work to do if he is to challenge his namesake!

gave them all sorts of corne in the straw, made great fires in the closes, and William Cooke, telling them there were billets & faggotts neerer to them than plough timber which they burned, they threatened to burne him, divers books, & writings of Consequence which were left in his study, they tore and burnt, & lighted Tobacco with them, & some they carried away to Whitelocke's extreme losse and prejudice, in his Estate, & in his profession loosing many excellent manuscripts of his fathers & others, & some of his own Labours, they brake down his Parke Pale, killed most of his deere though rascalls and carrions, and lett out the rest, only a Tame Hinde & his hounds they presented to Prince Rupert.

They eate and dranke up all that the house could afforde, brake up all the Trunks, chests, & places, any goods, linnen, or household stuffe that they could find, they carryed away, cutt the beds, lett out the feathers, & took away the tikes[28], the courtains, covers of chayres and stooles, his Coach and 4 good Coach horses, and all his saddle horses, & whatsoever they could lay their hands on they carried away or spoyled, & did all that malice & rapine could provoke barbarous mercenaries to commit, & so they left William Cooke & his company in the highest affright & detestation of them, that leudnes & damage could perswade him unto.

His smalle children att William Cooke's house had better usage, there Sir Thomas Byron[29] quartered, & asking whose children they were was anwseared that they were the children of a young woman there, William Cooke's daughter, butt he replied that they did not looke like her children, & wished them not to be afrayed to tell him whose children they were, for they should have no harme. They then confest they were Whitelocke's children their Landlord, & prayed that they might have no hurt done them, Sir Thomas sayed it were a barbarous thing to hurt those pretty innocent children, & kissed and made much

---

28 A strong cotton material, usually with stripes, that is used to cover bed mattresses or pillows.
29 Sir Thomas Byron was attacked by one of his own soldiers over a pay dispute in December 1643, and died from his wounds on 5 February 1644.

Chapter 3: Fawley Court

of them, & shewed great generosity towards Whitelocke whom they reputed their ennemy.

The house stood virtually derelict until 1684, when it was completely rebuilt. However, two stained glass windows were miraculously saved, and are now in Fawley Church.

25

Chapter 4

Greenlands

Greenlands House, within the parish of Hambleden, stands on the Thames almost exactly half way between Oxford (the location of King Charles' court) and London, and its position, being adjacent to the lock at Hambleden, meant it could control all movements along the river. It would be difficult to find a more strategically important location in the country – and, indeed, both warring factions recognised this. In an age when the state of the roads made them well-nigh impassable to heavy traffic – and were, in any case, vulnerable to hold-ups and looting – the Thames was a super highway, albeit a ponderously slow one. It was a vital artery for the transport of military equipment and material from London to Parliament's armies. Little wonder then that the Royalists identified Greenlands as one of a number of such houses surrounding Oxford as the city's first line of defence. As such, it would act as a base from which intelligence of troop and river movements could be gathered. Nor would its purpose be purely defensive; raiding parties could use it as a base to range far and wide harassing the enemy and engaging in their favourite game of 'beating up quarters'. This usually meant a troop of fast-moving light horsemen descending on a village in the early hours of the morning, hoping to catch enemy soldiers asleep in their billets, and killing or capturing as many as possible. The villagers of Hambleden would have been no strangers to soldiers continually moving about the area, foraging for food, drink, lodging, fodder for horses, wagons to carry their goods and anything else they wanted. Often they would leave their wounded to be cared for by the villagers. It made little difference which side you were on when undisciplined soldiers descended on you

In May 1644 Luke reported….

> ....Some of the enemies issued forth of Greenland House, and the Middlesex scouts light upon a party of them at Hambleton, where fourteen were taken prisoners and two killed.

No surprise then, that the Parliamentarians were determined that this Royalist outpost[30] had to be captured or destroyed. Such was its importance that no less a personage than the Earl of Essex himself[31] personally inspected the site in late 1643. Consequently, Whitelocke urged Essex to write to Parliament....

> ....that Greenland house was of great consequence, and thought a party should be sent from London to besiege it.

Parliament concurred and ordered in May 1644....

> ....That it be referred to the Committee of both Kingdoms, to take into Consideration the Garrison at Greenland House, for preventing them of doing Mischief to the Country.

Whitelocke, of course, couldn't wait to see the end of Greenlands. He....

> ....earnestly solicited the reducing of Greenland House, being a very ill neighbour to Fawley where his children were, & to his tenant William Cooke who was forced to pay 3d a week as a contribution.[32]

So, on his advice....

> ....the Lords and Commons took order to stop the passes between London and Oxford to prevent the King's Intelligence, and supplies of money and ammunition, whereof they understand he was in great want.

---

30 Sitting between Henley and Marlow – both Parliamentarian strongholds.
31 At the start of the Civil War, the Earl of Essex became the first Captain-General and Chief Commander of the Parliamentarian army. He was eventually overshadowed by the ascendancy of Oliver Cromwell and Thomas Fairfax, and resigned his commission in 1646.
32 To the fortification of Greenlands. A high payment, but Cooke was a tenant of Fawley Court Farm and Greenlands was perilously nearby.

Chapter 4: Greenlands

The siege of Greenlands was to become the most intense piece of military action in the Hambleden area in the Civil War. Contrary to popular notions that the Civil Wars were a succession of set piece clashes filled with dashing cavalry charges and tens of thousands of soldiers flinging themselves at each other, more typical were hundreds of skirmishes - collisions between foraging parties, attacks on convoys, sieges on country houses and castles. Most casualties were suffered in such clashes, which resembled low-level guerrilla warfare in areas not securely controlled by either side. Most house sieges were small affairs between handfuls of men and women who might have known each other in peacetime. They had to decide how to behave to each other now they were enemies, and feelings of betrayal were common. Nevertheless, such sieges were every bit as important as battles as they could control major routes – roads and rivers – and so help shape campaigns. The siege of Greenlands House on the Thames was just such a case.

Today, Greenlands house stands some way back from the Thames. It boasts lawns going down to the river, and it was on these lawns, on the bank of the river, that the original house stood. This aerial photo taken in the hot summer of 2022 might be its footprint. In a country that had undergone one of its longest periods of internal peace, the house's defences were generally in poor condition and, if they existed at all, tended to be medieval in origin. The house was nothing like the rather grand building that we see today, but much more like a medieval manor house – one large hall with a few outbuildings. Stables and farm buildings were in the foreground as was the custom in the later Middle Ages. It had been owned by the D'Oyley family for some 300 years. At the time of the Civil War it was in the possession of the Royalist, Sir John D'Oyley whose parents' fine memorial is in

29

Hambleden Church. The memorial shows ten children kneeling around their parents; those who pre-deceased their father are holding skulls, and the eldest two, John and James, are in Royalist costume, while the rest are dressed as Puritans, indicating dramatic and difficult divisions in the family's politics. It was the D'Oyley family that had changed the chief seat of Yewden Manor to Greenlands on acquiring it from Sir William Stonor back in the late fifteenth century.

Following the decision to garrison the house for the King, Luke's spies traced the inexorable build up of its defences. The following reports detail how Greenlands was converted by the Royalists from a country house to a fortified garrison during the winter of 1643 and the Spring of 1644. If some of the reports seem contradictory, that is the nature of espionage!

In December 1643 Luke received the first report of Greenlands being fortified. The engineers removed furnishings and other goods, to clear the way for their defensive works which, in the practice of the seventeenth century, initially comprised a circuit of earthen walls around the house with cannons positioned outside the defensive line to make assault dangerous and difficult.....

> ....Upon Friday last there went 500 horse and foote from Reading to Grinland and to Mr Dawley's house[33]. There they seysed upon all his goods, some of his goods they sent to Reading and the rest they keepe for their own uses for there is 300 foot quarter there this winter and 200 horse in Hambleden. They send for the countrymen to come to help to intrench Grinland. Yesterday there came 5 waggons loaden with ammunicon from Reading to Grinland.
>
> Upon Wednesday last a party of Reading forces pilledged Sir John Burlacy's[34] house at Bockmore and tooke away all that they layd their hands on.

---

33 Sir John D'Oyley
34 Borlase

Chapter 4: Greenlands

In December the Royalists began to fortify Greenlands....

> ....*The Kings horse intend to make a garrison of Marlowe and stop all the passage along the Thames[35]. They are making of bulwarkes at Greeneland howse and have warned in the contry to come and assist them and have planted 3 pieces of ordnance upon them. They are fortifying Greenland because they intend to stop all barges and prevent them from carrying billets and faggots and all manner of tymber to London. Wickham[36] is instructed to send every day 20 men for 4 dayes to help to make upp the works at Greenland*

Later in December the fortifications of Greenlands were consolidated....

> ....*there are noe soldiers at Henley but the townesmen and all thereabouts are making of bulwarkes at Greyes[37] and Greenland howse, where there are about 200 men, which cause the contry to bring in mony and provision.*

In January 1644....

> ....*they are still fortifieing of Greenland howse neere Henley and have pulled downe the roofe of the stables and other outhouwses, and are filling them upp with earth, and there are about 200 foote quartered in the howse.*

In February....

> ....*there is a troope of horse quartered in Henly under the command of Sir Charles Blunt. There are about 100 foote soldiers in Greeneland howse, which they have fortified and are now making bulwarkes to plant their ordnance upon. And they are commanded by Major Gilby.*

In March....

---
35 They didn't!
36 Wycombe
37 Greys Court

A Cruel Necessity – Hambleden and the Civil War

> ....There are about 100 foote and 50 horse at Greenland howse, and 2 small pieces, and the howse is very strongly fortified and they say there are two pieces of ordnance more to come thither from Oxford very suddenly. They report they make every weeke a loade of gunpowder, and have sent for workmen to make match.
>
> 1000 dragoones marcht out of Oxford under Sir Charles Blunt, to render assistance to Greenland howse, and the King sent out warrants the last weeke into Bucknghamshire to bring in men, money and arms to Greenland, and that those who refused are to bee plundered by the King's forces.
>
> 2 great iron pieces and as much ammunition as a barge could carry to be sent to Greenland.
>
> That at Greeneland house are not above 120 foote and that they force the contry thereabouts to send to his Majesty £200 monthly besides the maintenance of that garrison; that at Wallingford, Redding and Greenland are noe horse only Sir Charles Blunts troope which is not above 30 horse.

In May....

> ....Sir John Doyley fortified Greenlands for the King with 100 foot, but they have not above 30 muskets amongst them all. It is unclear whether they have 200 or 300 foot. They have 3 pieces of ordnance.

In fact, the Royalists had appointed Colonel Stephen Hawkins, *a very able soldier*, as Governor of Greenlands House on 15th May. He was instructed not to let the House fall into enemy hands, and to this end had been provided with sufficient ammunition and bread from Oxford. But not quite enough, for in early June a party from Greenlands was sent to Henley for replenishment. They were not lucky. As Luke reported from a member of the besieging forces....

> ....This morning we sent out a party of about 400 to Greenland House, and by 11 a clocke our Dragooners scouring before the Foot, entred Henley, and there found 7 Cavaliers, all well armed, collecting victuals and drinke; they discovered us not till we were in the

Chapter 4: Greenlands

Towne, but stood desperately to it, fired foure or five times apeece, and we having kil'd their Chaplaine (who refused quarter) they fled, at last we took a Lieutenant, an Ensigne, and two more, when they were falne back to Greenland House within twice musket shot. We desire but a reasonable helpe to send them packing, God send us faire weather: they are about 120, no horse, 4 or 5 pieces. I disarmed the Lieutenant, and tooke him alone, and shot one bullet of the two in the Priests body: he shot six times at us at foure yards distance, but hurt not a man of us, thanks be to God.

Nevertheless Hawkins felt so secure that on 18th June he felt able to warn the enemy forces before Greenlands House *to look to themselves, that they be not surprised.*

Setting the heavy cannon and digging the earthworks and trenches required an experienced engineer and was a slow and laborious business. The fortifications were designed to protect against cannon fire and make any assault dangerous and difficult. Once fixed they could not easily be moved, so Hawkins had to take a bit of a gamble in anticipating the possible direction of attack. I suspect that as any assault was expected to come from the north, the cannon and other defences were aimed inland, i.e. away from the river. A decision Colonel Hawkins would come to regret.

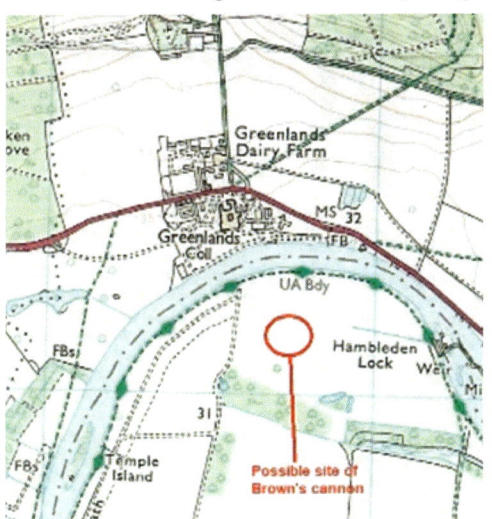

We can imagine the hills and woods above and around Greenlands being full of besieging Parliamentarians so that the only way in and out of the garrison was by river. There was, in fact, never going to be a full-on assault – the troops were only there to prevent any escapees from the house. Parliamentarian guns had been set up on the other side of the Thames, to devastating effect. We can only imagine how the guardians of Greenlands must have felt as they watched the ponderous, inexorable columns of heavy ox carts and militia heaving artillery into the fields on the other side of the river. Luke reported in June….

> ….we have planted three of our biggest Sacres within musket shot of the House, and yesterday we sent them 30 shot, which much shattered the house, and amazed the garrison that were in it, our forces that are before it, are (blessed be God) in an healthfull condition, though wee are forced to continue our watchings very strictly, and sometimes can get little or no rest for seven nights together, we have before the house above 300 Foot, under the command of Lieutenant Colonell Bradley, which came from Windsor, besides 400 Foot which we have in Henley, our Horse not being above 150 and under the command of Captaine Terrill, Captaine Nash and Captaine Aldridge. The Governour of Greenland House is Colonell Stephen Hawkins, who is Landlord of Bishops Court in the Old Bayly, he lately sent out about an hundred to fall upon our Quarters, but they were soon beat in, and two of them killed.

All the besiegers had to do was wait, and in time the garrison would run out of supplies and would have to surrender. But Essex could not wait, so in June 1644 the experienced Major-General Brown, who only two years previously had been a coal and timber trader in London, [38] was instructed by Parliament to destroy the House….

> ….to do any other Thing whatsoever, as to him shall seem requisite, for the infesting and destroying of….the Fort[39] of Greenland House, and Parts adjacent…

and to march *with great strength* against Greenlands.

The soldiers made a forced march all night from Aylesbury to Wycombe where they rested on the 10th of July, news being brought to Brown that the enemy were gathering in force to prevent him reaching Greenlands. After

---

38 Sometimes spelled Browne. He was knighted in 1660; he later became Lord Mayor of London.
39 Note the word 'fort'.

Chapter 4: Greenlands

much sweating and muttering[40] as they trudged up the hill from Wycombe, they reached Medmenham where they rested at the site of the Dog and Badger[41] before being ferried across the river. They arrived opposite Greenlands on the 11th without obstruction, and *drawing up my main body, faced the house, firing a few shots with our gun, which did good execution.*

Whitelocke takes up the story….

> *….The Lords sent to the Commons that a Regiment or more of foote or more might be sent to joyne with the forces then before Greenland-house & that they might batter it from the other side of the Thames. Greenland-house was besieged, their batteries planted on the further side of the river Thames, yet near the house, against which they made many shot[42] and much battered it.*
>
> *The besiegers of Greenland-house had almost beaten the house about the ears of the garrison. A party from Oxford and Wallingford came to relieve Greenland-house; whereupon the parliament force drew off to Henley[43], and the King's forces brought their fellows little relief, only carried away 29 women and some plunder, and so returned, and so the besiegers sat down again before it.*

They must have known it was all over. From such a close range, the besiegers could barely miss. It was a slow death. The rate of cannon-fire of the heavy Sakers[44] and the lighter Drakes was ponderous. The process of sponging-out and reloading was deliberate and complex. Powder was kept in small budge barrels near the guns, which were fired by the application of linstock to the touch-hole. After the cannon had been fired the soldiers

---

40 No cursing or blaspheming as they were all good, God-fearing Puritans. I wonder!
41 They must have left some ordnance behind, as a cannonball was found when the pub underwent reconstruction in 1845.
42 Portions of the foundations have been uncovered from time to time, and cannon balls, relics of the siege, can still be found in the area to this day..
43 It seems strange that a relieving part should be permitted into the House.
44 About 3¼ inch bore, 5¼ pounder.

operating it had to go through a strict procedure of cleaning, reloading the weapon and loading the gunpowder before it could be fired again. The risk of premature explosions was very great, and it is doubtful whether it was possible to fire more than one round every three minutes.

In September, only two months later, the house *could no longer be defended, the whole structure being beaten down by the cannon*, so, by order of the King, the Governor of Greenlands, a shell-shocked Colonel Hawkins surrendered *the house and fort of Greenland upon honourable terms*. These were:

> *1. That Collonel Hawkins shall deliver up to Major Browne, for the use of the Parliament, the House and Fort of Greenland House, with all the Ammunition, Ordnance and provision therein, in the same condition that it is in at this present.*

> *2. That all the Officers shall quietly march forth of the said House, with their horses and swords, and the common souldiers and Canoniers, with their Armes and Coloures, viz, swords, Pikes, and Pistols.*

> *3. That the said Major Generall do allow them a Convoy of Horse to Nettlebed (about three miles thence) which are to return again within six houres, without any molestation of the said forces so conveyed.*

> *4. That the said Major Generall shall cause to be provided for the said Offisers and souldiers, two Teames and Carts, to carry away their Baggage, and such provision as is necessary for their journey to Wallingford, which Carts and Horses are to be returned so soon as they come thither.*

> *5. That all prisoners taken on either side be forth discharged.*

These terms seem remarkably generous, though perhaps not unusual particularly as Brown had suffered minimal losses during the action. The rules of siege were well known to participants. After the defence had put up a good fight, they could then demand a 'parley' and bargain upon the terms of surrender. If they capitulated, they were spared; if they refused to surrender, they were likely to be stormed and massacred.

As was common practice, after the surrender Brown looted the house as his reward for the victory. It was said that he found five pieces of brass ordnance, thirty barrels of gunpowder, a great store of bullet and match, a good quantity of cheese, biscuits, fish, malt, flour, beer, oats, peas, and *a great plenty of household stuff*.

He wrote for instructions, whether to demolish the house or leave it standing, but getting impatient at not receiving an answer, he acceded to the general wish of the countryside and commenced to 'slight' or destroy the fortifications. Too late he received instructions to garrison Greenlands against a possible siege, *if the enemy should look that way*. The gunpowder had already been used to raze the house. The blast could be heard as far away as Henley. Farmers in Hambleden heard the explosion, and couldn't get down to the house quick enough to view the spectacle and gather what plunder they could after Brown's troops had scoured the site. Over two hundred people gathered – an enormous number for such a spontaneous event, prepared to risk life and limb among falling timbers and burning embers and with minor explosions of ordnance still a possibility. Some emerged from the ruin grinning and clasping a 'valuable', most drifted home empty handed.

Whitelocke was dismayed that he was unable to recover the goods that had been pillaged from Fawley Court and taken to Greenlands some months earlier....

> *....Many of Whitelockes goods were in Greenland house when it was rendered by Hawkins the then Governour, which goods the Parlement soldiers tooke, & sold in Henley & in the Countrey, & none of them were restored to Whitelocke though they were known to be his, & that he was a Parlement man, & designed to commaund that party. Brown would not help him uppon complaint to him, butt had learned so much of the Martial law as to answear Whitelocke that*

> when the enemy had taken these goods, then Whitelockes property was gone, & now the Parlement soldiers had taken them from the ennemy, they were lawfull prize to them, so loath was he to displease the soldiers, or backward to doe right to Whitelocke who had his goods thus injuriously detained from him by those of his own party.

In October 1651 Whitelocke purchased Greenlands from the D'Oyleys for £6,500 thus consolidating his Thameside properties from Greenlands to Henley.

Chapter 5

Henley and Phyllis Court

In 1642, as now, Henley was the commercial centre favoured by the villagers of Hambleden. It was a market town then as it is today; in fact, it has held regular markets since the 13th century. Every Thursday the road to Henley was full of farmers, some with carts of grain, others herding sheep and cattle[45] to the town, and returning with provisions. They left the Market Place awash with the blood of butchered animals. It was also a bustling riverside port, with grain, timber and firewood being sent to London. The river front was crammed with wharves, granaries, warehouses and boat builders – all thirsty trades! Little wonder that the town became known for the malting of barley and the brewing of beer.

The town was agreeably compact - this detail from *Landscape with Rainbow* by Jan Siberechts painted in 1690 gives us some idea of how tightly packed the buildings were. It extended from Friday Street in the south to the manor, now

Phyllis Court[46], in the north and took in Hart Street and New Street. To the west it included Bell Street and the Market Place. Within that small area it has been estimated that there were at least

---
45 There were 12 butchers in the town.
46 There has been a house on this site, called Fillets Court, dating back to the 14th century. The name was gradually corrupted to Phyllis Court - the name Fillets derives from an Old English name for hay, and may originally have referred to the nearby meadows.

twenty-five more alehouses than today. No need to go thirsty in Henley; we can only imagine how much money the farmers of Hambleden didn't take back for their wives on market day! The town was not the rather genteel place it is today (home of the Henley **Royal** Regatta), but rather a rough, tough, dirty, hard drinking place as befits all ports. The removal of dung (human and animal) from the streets was a continual problem. Fines were levied against the owners of livestock wandering in the streets. In 1620 the town's streets were *much broken, worn and annoyed with great holes*, which was blamed on the turning of carts carrying corn, grain and malt to and from weekly barges. Inhabitants were ordered to park their carts lengthways along the street, and to use planks to help with loading. Even so, in 1661 rutted streets tipped over Whitelocke's coach, throwing his wife *into a dirty hole*. No surprise then when Whitelocke, as Justice of the Peace, recorded that the townsmen *gave him great trouble by their*

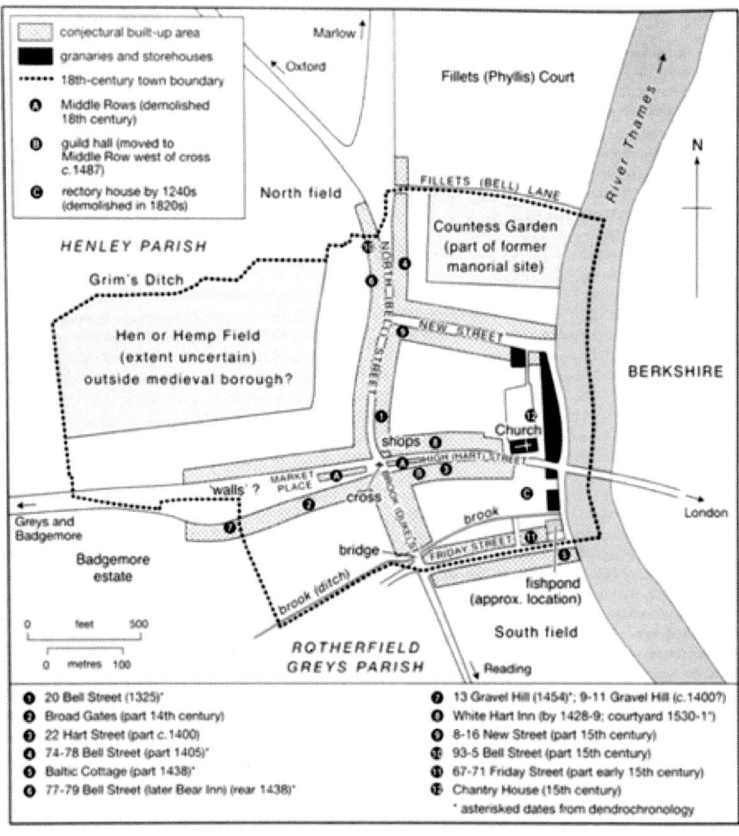

Chapter 5: Henley and Phyllis Court

multitude of people, & too many of them idle and disorderly. The further north one lived, towards the manor, the more salubrious it became.

Henley suffered at the hands of both parties in the Civil War. Its position between London and Oxford made the town strategically important. Control of the river was considered essential: Parliamentarian scouts reported that provisions were sometimes surreptitiously shipped upstream to Henley for conveyance to Oxford by cart or river.

At the start of the war the people of Henley seem to have been either divided over their loyalties or possibly just resigned to events as they happened – like most folk everywhere they merely wished to get on with their lives accepting whoever was in charge. Henley was their home, always had been and always would be. They needed no justification for being there, no creed or warped ideology to excuse their existence. All they wanted to do was get on with their thriving corn markets and malting kilns. Initially it was the Royalists, under

Prince Rupert, the King's nephew, who held the town, taking over the Bell Inn[47] at Northfield End for use as their base. Prince Rupert was a flamboyant, inspiring leader, the archetypal Cavalier; despite his youth he had wide experience of continental warfare (he was born in Prague, the son of the German Prince Frederick V of the Palatinate), and was a keen student of military theory. His daring and skill gave victory to the Royalist horse in most of the early battles of the Civil Wars. However, he had an unenviable reputation during the war as a merciless and inhuman slaughterer[48], so Henley got off lightly as the town

---

47 The most prestigious inn in Henley, owned by Whitelocke. Archbishop Laud stayed there in 1633.
48 The accusation was not hard to make as he was in command of the perpetrators of massacres at Birmingham, Bolton and Leicester. Estimates for the dead at Bolton range from 200 up to 1,800. Even the lower figure would make Bolton the worst massacre of the war.

was not sacked. Whitelocke's house at Fawley Court did not get off so leniently, and was ransacked by Royalist troops, a *Tame Hinde & hounds* confiscated for Prince Rupert. During the occupation of the town, Prince Rupert is reputed to have had a spy from the Parliamentarian side hanged on an elm tree in front of the Bell Inn, a tree that became known as Rupert's Elm.[49] A local resident recalled….

> ….*When I was a boy I could see the chain they did it with. It was a winter's day, with snow on the ground, and he looked like a crow dangling black, there, under the bare branches.*

Nether the Bell Inn nor the tree still exist. The Bell Inn subsequently became the home of Henley Grammar School and was later converted into private houses.[50] The elm tree survived for another 350 years but finally succumbed to the effects of age and Dutch elm disease. It was felled in 1995 and its stump removed. A piece of this historic tree can be seen in the River and Rowing Museum in Henley.

There were several skirmishes in and around Henley, typical of which was the following….

> ….*Towards [yesterday] evening it was certified, that Sir Arth. Aston*[51] *Governour of Reading, understanding that a certaine number of the Rebels were gotten into Henley on the Thames, and began to fortifie; sent thither his Sergeant Major with some*

---

49 Several buildings around the site of the elm have included the prince's name in their name, such as Rupert House School. Why so many buildings have chosen to be associated with such a controversial individual who was no friend to Henley is a bit of a mystery.

50 A house called Rupert's Elm is still there today behind high walls, directly opposite the store on the other side of the road at the confluence of Bell Street, the Fairmile and the Henley/Marlow road at Northfield End. In the cellar is a bricked-up door facing Bell Street which conceals a tunnel that at one time went under the road. A message is written on one of the rafters in the roof so somebody was perhaps concealed up there.

51 Aston was most unpopular due to his severity and short temper He broke his leg in a riding accident in 1644, gangrene set in and it required amputation. It was replaced by a wooden leg. In 1648 he was made Governor of Drogheda in Ireland. Besieged in 1649 by the New Model Army led by Cromwell, Drogheda was stormed with notoriously little quarter given. Sir Arthur's brains were beaten out with his own wooden leg, which the Parliamentarian soldiers falsely suspected was full of gold coins.

Chapter 5: Henley and Phyllis Court

companies to remove them thence, who charged to furiously upon them, that he killed many of them, and gained their Ordnance. But being ingaged too farre amongst them, and not well seconded by his men, he was most unfortunately slaine: on which unluckie accident, the residue not having any to command them, retreated backe to Reading, from whence they came, without more losse them onely of the Sergeant Major.

Early in 1643, the Parliamentarians took the town which the King had neglected to garrison. Henley would remain in Parliamentarian control until the end of the war. More skirmishes followed as the Royalists attempted to retake the town, the most famous of which was the so-called Battle of Duke Street.[52] Sir Arthur Ashton launched an attack from the direction of Reading. A Parliamentarian supporter had sent word of the attack so the Roundhead army under the command of Samuel Turner, were ready. A cannon was placed in Duke Street, which was only as wide as a carriage in 1643. Once the Royalists were in the street, there was no escape. When the dust settled, four Royalists lay dead as well as five horses. Two soldiers died of their wounds the following day.

The parliamentary soldiers did much damage to the town, plundering and looting. Many suffered, but perhaps none more so than Whitelocke. In March 1644 they set the Bell on fire, just over the wall from Phyllis Court. Whitelocke's faithful servant, William Cooke, wrote to his master and mistress….

….Upon Wenday nite there hapined a nill mischance at the Bell at Henley about two of the clocke in the morning by fire. It began at the Yalhouse, as we go to Filles Court. There is not much of the timber destroyed but the tiles be distroid, the selling bet down, the walls bet down, the women's household stuff torn and lost to pieces of her great loss but she doth umbelie you that you would be pleased to set you helping hand to mend it.

I am very willing to have it mended again, and had thought to set upon it without troubling you. I have take a nottis of it, about 2 thousens

---

52 Then known as Duck Street.

> *of tiles will heale it again, so that I thing that the charge will amount to fiftie pounds to mend it if it be suddenlie done fiftie pounds will do more now than a hundred will do twelve months hence, and therefore if I do not hear from you to the contrar I will set upon it, to mend it, that I will have it du within this month if God will give me leafe.*[53]

Whitelocke was furious….

> *….as some supposed it was done by the Carelesnes of some Parlement soldiers quartered there,*

Phyllis Court was also ransacked….

> *….& they att Phyllis Court did him much spoyle and mischief, though he was a Parlement man, but brutish soldiers make no distinction.*

> *Major General Skippon directed Phyllis Court to be made a Garryson, & it was regularly fortefyed and strong & well manned, because Greenland, hard by it, was a Garryson for the King, and betwixt these two Garrysons stood Whitelocke's house at Fawley Court, miserably torn & plundered by each of them.*[54]

Skippon set about converting the house from an impressive rambling Tudor mansion[55], surrounded by fine trees and parkland, heated by many fires[56] and well lit by many windows, to a fort. It already had a moat and a drawbridge and so was ideal as a garrison.[57] This image is of the north view of Phyllis Court as it was after the Civil War fortifications were built.

---

53 It is interesting to note that a countryman like William Cook could read and write. If you read the passage out loud you will get a flavour of the local accent at the time.
54 Fawley Court was uninhabitable, so despite its sacking, Phyllis Court became the main residence for Whitelocke and his family. It became the local HQ of the Earl of Essex.
55 The original building on this site dates from 1301. It was the Manor house of Henley-on-Thames and was known as Fillets Court. Queen Anne, the consort of King James I, visited the house in 1604.
56 In the 1660's it was taxed on 17 hearths.
57 The Phyllis Court website records that 'In 1643, Oliver Cromwell used the site as a garrison during the Civil War and built the wall, known today as Cromwell's Wall, from the rubble of the destroyed Manor house'.

Chapter 5: Henley and Phyllis Court

The almost Lowry-like image[58] depicts soldiers going about their routine patrols or manning the deadly cannons above the heavily spiked walls of the defences. The large house behind them looks very welcoming, with smoke billowing out of various chimneys. It evokes images of reclining in comfortable chairs next to the warmth of a cosy fireplace, all set within the charms of a peaceful and calm woodland, with flocks of birds flying around above them. Curiously, standing on the drawbridge next to one of the soldiers and dressed in the same uniform, is a smaller person who only reaches the height of the soldier's waist. This child must have been one of Whitelocke's sons – perhaps the last person one would expect to see in a garrison in time of war.

Skippon diverted the Thames to increase the size of the existing moat[59], and garrisoned the house with cannon, 300 soldiers and a troop of horse. Whitelocke was pleased to note that….

> ….*The great guns about it were very good & usefull, & the officers and soldiers were stout men and well armed.*

In April 1643 Reading fell to the Parliamentarians[60] and gradually discipline

---

58 Watercolour drawing by R. Shennan, 1786, copied from the original and inscribed to Strickland Freeman, owner of Phyllis Court. Original was found under panelling at Phyllis Court and was of early 18th century.
59 The moat is now connected to the river and used for as a mooring for boats.
60 3,300 Royalist troops who were stationed in Reading were besieged by 19,000 Parliamentary militia. The siege lasted twelve days until a truce was agreed, and the Royalists retreated to Oxford.

was introduced to their soldiers, so by 1646 Whitelocke felt it safe to dismantle the fortifications at Phyllis Court[61]. He....

> ....*sent in workemen with Pickaxes and shovels for the dismanteling of the Garryson of Henley and Phyllis Court, & Cartes to be imployed about that gratefull worke.*
>
> *A great many of the Countrey came in to Whitelocke with mattocks, shovels & some with Teemes to help in slighting of Phyllis Court Garrison, & Whitelocke sett his soldiers to work in it & allowed them 6d a day for it besides their wages, the Countrey paid their own men, he threw down the Breastworks & made hansom walks of them on two sides, digged down the Bulworkes, sent away the Great guns and ammunition. He caused the lines to be digged down, the grafts filled, the drawbridge to be pulled up and all levelled.*

In the town, the turnpikes were removed, the bridge repaired and made a free thoroughfare. The relief to the people of Henley and surrounding villages from the presence of the rough soldiers, the terrible quarterly money assessments, the requisitions, the ever-present dread of plundering, must have been enormous.

Peaceful relations between former combatants must have been restored in Henley as Whitelocke records that on July 13, 1647....

> .... *Newes came to Whitelocke that the next day the King intended to come to Bowles att Henley, & to dine with Whitelocke at Phyllis Court, but he, to avoid jealousy, went this evening towards London & left his house att the Kings service, and thus he was quiet in no place neither att London nor in the Countrey.*

This is a curious event. Even though peace might have broken out in the town, Charles must have been taking a bit of a risk to go to what was a former Parliamentarian stronghold for a game of bowls, with the expectation of dining

---

61 In 1688, Whitelock's eldest son by his second marriage, William Whitelocke, entertained William III at Phyllis Court while on his triumphal journey from Torbay to London. It was there that he held his first court and received a loyal declaration from Peers and an address from the Corporation of London.

afterwards with Whitelocke, a Parliamentarian, albeit a moderate one. He was on the run at the time, having slipped away under cover of darkness from Hampton Court where he was being held under house arrest. Whitelocke was wise to distance himself from the visit, and take refuge in London.

Chapter 6

Afterwards

On Sunday January 31st 1649 the village of Hambleden woke up to a new world. If they had found the events of the past seven years perplexing, they could never have imagined this. The public nature of the King's trial and execution invited public judgement and debate, and Hambleden was happy to oblige. There was little enthusiasm for attending church as bewildered folks stood around sharing their views on what life without a King, power or religion held in store for them. For generations they had been content to be seduced by the mystery of the crown. Who now would keep them safe? Who would stop the soldiers burning and pillaging and allow them to sleep quietly in their beds? Who would protect them from the wars and politics which seemed to go on and on? Who would save them from anarchy? Would their futures be subject entirely to the power of the sword? What will happen to the King's son, Charles, the presumptive heir to the throne?

There was little outward enthusiasm for the execution of the King. Perhaps some of the villagers understood the necessity for the bloody act; perhaps some were so committed to the puritan crusade that they couldn't envisage life without it. In any case, all were fearful for the future - terrified of what God might bring upon their heads for such an unnatural assault upon their very being. To them, the wrath of God was not an abstract concept, or something to be encountered only in the afterlife, but was starkly real and visible daily in acts of divine justice such as the awful weather. It was as if their world had turned upside down. Nothing would ever be the same again.

It was a poor and hungry world - the war had meant that food production had more or less broken down. Fields had been neglected, several having been trampled flat by many boots and horses' hooves. The transportation of food was hit by the destruction of roads and bridges. Consequently, much grain went unmilled. On top of this, recent harvests had been terrible; the price of bread and meat were rising faster than wages. Normal life expectancy among even the nobility averaged under 30 years of age for males between 1650 and 1675. Disease may have carried off over 100,000 people in England between 1640 and 1652. For ordinary people, there were also the financial contributions levied by both sides and the substantial increase in parliamentary taxation: propositions, 'loans', weekly taxes, 'fifth and twentieth', the excise and so on were far more onerous than anything Charles I had ever attempted prior to 1642.

That is not to say that everyone suffered during the war. As in any war, there are opportunities to make money by selling to the armies of whatever hue. In Hambleden, the blacksmiths, leather workers, wheelwrights, carpenters and bread makers all found a ready market for their services. And, of course, Hambleden would have enjoyed its fair share of bribery and corruption. So, when discharged soldiers from both sides began to filter back into the village, it took some time for grudges and suspicions to be forgotten. Perhaps some never were. But all hands were needed to rebuild the local economy – prepare the fields, repair barns, care for the maimed and disfigured. At the end of the day, farmers don't care what Government they live under, so long as they can plough and go to market. Former enemies were soon intermarrying, and split families making up – a testament to the solidity of the community.

But now the country was ruled, not by those who had released the country from a tyrannical King in favour of a democratic Parliament, but by Christian fundamentalists who now had to think through the implications of a kingless constitution – what today we might call regime change. Their motivation was not political, to offer liberty to free-born Englishman, but religious, to pursue jihad against all Catholics and sympathisers with a fanatical obsession. As Cromwell put it....

> *Religion was not the thing at first contested for but God brought it to that issue at last; and gave it unto us by redundancy, and at last it proved that which was most dear to us.*

Chapter 6: Afterwards

They wanted to search out anybody who might be having a good time and put a stop to it at once. In June 1647, the feast days of Christmas, Easter and Whitsun were all abolished by Parliament. Christmas was deemed to be a time of fasting and humiliation instead of the century's old religious festival and holiday period that we enjoy today. Like now, the season was marked with the exchanging of gifts, feasting, carol singing, eating mince pies and general merriment. Also, in common with today, this often led to over-indulgence and sometimes drunkenness, excesses that were strongly contradictory to sober Puritan values. Those who celebrated and enjoyed themselves were sinfully *giving liberty to carnal and sensual delights*. In London, soldiers patrolled the streets and took by force any food being cooked for a Christmas celebration when people should have been fasting. Traditional decorations like holly and ivy were banned and singing carols was outlawed. Even the word itself was banned, suggesting as it did, a form of mass. A popular Royalist ballad bemoaned....

> *To conclude, I'll tell you news that's right,*
> *Christmas was killed at Naseby fight:*
> *Charity was slain at that same time,*
> *Jack Tell-truth too, a friend of mine,*
> *Likewise, then did die, roast beef and shred pie,*
> *Pig, Goose and Capon no quarter found.*
> *Yet let's be content, and the times lament,*
> *You see the world turned upside down.*

Fines were imposed for sporting activities, for swearing, gambling and excessive drinking as countless pubs were closed down. Even the private business of sex was adjudged to be sinful if it was enjoyed. In fact, this was the most sexually repressive regime in our history, making adultery a capital offence.

In 1650 Parliament passed 'An Act for the Suppressing of the Detestable Sins of Incest, Adultery and Fornication'. A passage read....

> .... *For the suppressing of the abominable and crying sins of Incest, Adultery and Fornication, wherewith this Land is much defiled, and Almighty God highly displeased; Be it Enacted by the Authority of this present Parliament, That if any person or persons whatsoever,*

> *shall from and after the Four and twentieth day of June, in the year of our Lord One thousand six hundred and fifty, Marry, or have the carnal knowledge of the Body of his or her Grandfather or Grandmother, Father or Mother, Brother or Sister, Son or Daughter, or Grandchilde, Fathers Brother or Sister, Mothers Brother or Sister, Fathers Wife, Mothers Husband, Sons Wife, Daughters Husband, Wives Mother or Daughter, Husbands Father or Son; all and every such Offences are hereby adjudged and declared Incest: And every such Offence shall be, and is hereby adjudged Felony; and every person offending therein, and confessing the same, or being thereof convicted by verdict upon Indictment or Presentment, before any Judge or Justices at the Assize or Sessions of the Peace, shall suffer death as in case of Felony, without benefit of Clergy.[62]*

Fighting cocks, bears and dogs were slaughtered, not to spare the wretched animals, but to prevent them giving any pleasure to spectators. Banned were maypole dancing, revellings at country weddings and traditional Saint's Day activities including the St Bartholomew's Day Fair in Hambleden. The country was now a Protectorate, governed by a Protestant version of the Taliban. Willing helpers were recruited as 'commissioners' to identify anyone guilty of lewdness, playing cards, encouraging traditional pastimes or scoffing at the godly. In Hambleden, one Thomas Begg was arrested as a 'delinquent' and ordered to pay a fine of £10. These commissioners were supported by the army who believed they were an army of saints who were possessed by the Holy Spirit and were thus assured of their own salvation.. They believed that they had been victorious in battle because God had been in the midst of them. *"If God be for us,"* ran the text from Romans 8:31, *"who can be against us?"* In short, England had become a police state.

Witchcraft was punished with great severity. For generations people had been turning to 'wise women' for protection against pain and illness and early death, against fire and dearth, for magical cures and love potions, for help in the recovery of stolen goods or missing children. They were part of the fabric of village life. Now witch-finders roamed the country. Every old woman with

---

[62] It makes one wonder what on earth went on beforehand!

a wrinkled face, a furrowed brow, a hairy lip, gaps in her teeth, a squint eye, wearing ragged clothes and a dog or cat by her side was under suspicion.

In Hambleden, Rector Roberts was extruded[63] and replaced by a Mr Henry Goodyer, described as a 'Minister of the Gospel'. He preached that....

> ...*forty years were the English under the government of two Scottish kings, which is just as many years as the children of Israel did wander in the wilderness before they came unto rest.*

The parish was not convinced. With no bishops to govern the nation's religion, many feared the country would be engulfed by a tide of irreligion and ungodliness. Orders to replace the now traditional Book of Common Prayer with a 'Directory of Public Worship' were resisted.

All in all, it was not a happy time. It could not last, and in fact, it didn't. Within eleven years of the execution of Charles l, the throne was restored to his son Charles ll. The Restoration was greeted as deliverance from a world of confusion; it was a reminder of the British natural mistrust of religious ideologues and zealots, and that protracted political conflict left most people weary and perplexed. Never again would the country be ruled by generals. That the United Kingdom remains a monarchy to this day is due in no small part to the events and experiences of the Civil War and the Interregnum.

Henry Goodyer made way for the restored Rector Roberts, and a year later by Rector Sebastian Smith. Elizabeth, dowager Countess of Sunderland continued to live in Hambleden Manor until her death in 1654; thereafter the Manor passed to Thomas Savage, 3rd Earl Rivers. A cousin of the Countess' late husband, Adrian Scrope of Wormsley, had been one of the fifty-nine signatories of Charles' death warrant. On the Restoration he was arrested for treason and hanged, drawn and quartered at Charing Cross. As a special favour, his body was returned to his family for burial, rather than being put on display as was the usual practice for the bodies of executed traitors.

---

63 He returned to the village in 1660.

John D'Oyley, like other Royalists, was heavily fined for his support of the King and was forced to sell the Greenland Estate, together with the Manor of Yewden and his other lands in Hambleden. It was bought by Whitelocke in 1651 for £6,500. He was later elected MP for Oxford, and died in 1660.

Whitelocke had abhorred death of the King – on the day of the King's execution, he wrote that….

> ….*I went not to the House, but stayed all day at home in my study and at my prayers, in the hopes that this day's work might not so displease God as to bring prejudice to this poor afflicted nation.*

He suffered another tremendous blow when his beloved wife, Frances, died in 1649. He spent time looking for a new wife – someone who would be kind to his ten children. He found such a person in Mary Wilson and they married in Autumn 1650. Five more sons and two daughters followed. He became a commissioner of the Great Seal[64] in 1648 and was elected to the Council of State on the formation of the Commonwealth in 1649. During the next 10 years he served three additional terms as commissioner of the Great Seal.

He ceased to be a member of Parliament in 1659, having been a member since 1641.[65] In 1653 he was sent as Ambassador to Sweden, returning to Fawley in 1660 with the Restoration. His reputation for moderation - viewed by many as political vacillation - saved him from prosecution after the Restoration. He was, however, fined £900 for his support of the Parliamentarians. He manged to pay £500 and was obliged to sell Fawley Court and Henley Park to raise the balance. He lived out his last years in rather reduced circumstances, and died in 1675, a much disillusioned man. He had walked a tightrope between the two warring parties during the War – he described himself as *industriously labouring to promote all overtures for peace.* He had been one of eight commissioners sent by Parliament to the King at Oxford in January and March 1643 to explore the possibility of some form of reconciliation. He believed that there was a rational point of balance and that political life would naturally bend towards it. He found instead that a 'natural' centre ground was a delusion, that politics was

---

64 Equivalent to the Lord Chancellor.
65 Apart from a few months in 1643, during The Barebones Parliament.

Chapter 6: Afterwards

not a reasonable science but a hot, murky, passionate struggle for power – that righteousness had triumphed over reasonableness.

In 1675 he died at Chilton Lodge at Leverton in Berkshire which had been purchased with his third wife's fortune in 1663, and was buried modestly and without ostentation in Fawley Church. His biographer, Ruth Spalding, describes him as 'highly intelligent, musical, flamboyant, very loving, of an independent mind, and a staunch defender of freedom'.

An epitaph that perhaps we might all aspire to.

Postscript

A thought-provoking observation about the war was suggested by Bertrand Russell in 1929....

> ....*Puritanism so disgusted the mass of ordinary citizens that they have never again allowed it to control the Government. The Puritans, persecuted in England, colonised New England, and subsequently the Middle West. The American Civil War was a continuation of the English Civil War, the Southern States having been mainly colonised by opponents of the Puritans. But unlike the English Civil War, it led to a permanent victory of the Puritan Party. The result is that the greatest Power in the world is controlled by men who inherit the outlook of Cromwell's Ironsides.*
>
> SCEPTICAL ESSAYS

Appendix 1

Timeline

1629   King Charles l ascends the throne of England, Scotland & Ireland

1630   Death of Emanuel Scrope, 1st Earl of Sunderland, 11th Baron Scrope of Bolton, owner of Hambleden Manor

1632   King Charles reportedly stays at Red Lion in Henley

1633   Archbishop Laud stays at Bell Inn, Henley

1634   Death of Rebecca, Sir Bulstrode Whitelocke's first wife.

       Whitelocke meets and subsequently marries Frances Willoughby

1640   Rector Roberts replaces Rector Danelaw in Hambleden

1642   Cavalier detachment in Skirmett

       King Charles attempts to arrest five MPs

       King Charles again in Henley, accompanied by Prince Rupert

       King Charles raises his standard in Nottingham; the Civil War has begun

1643   Greenlands House fortified

       Fawley Court sacked

       Battle of Duke Street in Henley

1644   Phyllis Court sacked

       Greenlands besieged and sacked

A Cruel Necessity – Hambleden and the Civil War

1646   King spends a night in Hambleden Manor

       Phyllis Court fortifications dismantled

1648   Whitelocke becomes a Commissioner of the Great Seal

1649   King executed. Country governed as a Commonwealth.

       Frances, Whitelocke's wife, dies

1650   Whitelocke marries Mary Wilson, his third wife.

       Minister Henry Goodyer replaces Rector Roberts as minister for Hambleden

1651   Whitelocke purchases Greenlands from the D'Oyleys.

1653   Whitelocke sent as Ambassador to Sweden.

1654   Death of Elizabeth, Dowager Countess of Sunderland

1660   Crown restored to Charles ll

       Whitelocke returns from Sweden

       Rector Roberts restored in Hambleden

1661   Rector Sebastian Smith installed at Hambleden

1675   Death of Whitelocke.

Appendix 2

Dramatis Personae

Sir Bulstrode Whitelocke – resident of Fawley Court

Earl of Essex – Commander of Parliamentary army

Sir Samuel Luke – Spymaster for the Earl of Essex

Emanuel Scrope – owner of Hambleden Manor

Elizabeth, Dowager Countess of Sunderland – resident of Hambleden Manor

Charles I – King of England

Rector George Roberts – Rector of Hambleden at outbreak of Civil War

Minister Henry Goodyer – Minister of Hambleden during the Interregnum

Rebecca Whitelocke – first wife of Sir Bulstrode Whitelocke

William Cooke – servant of Sir Bulstrode Whitelocke

Frances Willoughby – second wife of Sir Bulstrode Whitelocke

Lord Willoughby – brother of Frances Willoughby

Earl Rutland – uncle of Frances Willoughby

Sir John Byron – commander of Royalist forces at Fawley Court

Sir Thomas Byron – Sir John's brother

Sir John D'Oyley – owner of Greenlands House

Sir Charles Blunt – responsible for the fortification of Greenlands House

Sir Stephen Hawkins – Governor of Greenland House

Major General Brown – commander of siege of Greenlands

Prince Rupert – commander of Royalist forces in Henley

Oliver Cromwell – the senior commander in the Parliamentarian army and later a politician. He ruled as Lord Protector from December 1653 until his death in September 1658.

Appendix 3

Cormorants and Lovebirds

As we have noted, the most important man in the area in 1642 was Sir Bulstrode Whitelocke, a widower and owner of Phyllis Court, Fawley Court and several properties in Henley. Although not directly related to the Civil War, the story of how he pursued Frances Willoughby of Hambleden Manor to be his second wife is quite charming and worth relating here. The following are extracts from his diary.

After the death of his first wife, Rebecca, in 1634, Whitelocke ….

> ….*removed with his childe to Fawley Court where he recreated himselfe in fishing with Cormorants*[66]*, for which sport he had made a pond, & an arche of bricke, with a Banquetting House*[67] *upon it of costly flint worke which stood neer the Thames, & had a fayre gravell walke from the house unto it.*

But the banqueting house was not to last long….

> ….*Whither through the default of the workmen, or of the foundation, is not acknowledged, butt soon after he had finished this building,*

---

66 Popular in England during the 16th to 17th centuries.
67 To be used as an office for meetings as well as for festivities.

the Arche began to fayle, & the building uppon it to cracke⁶⁸, so that he was faine, as the lesse inconvenience to take down the banqueting house, & rebuilt it on higher ground, adjoining to his Orchard. The banqueting house, though butt 12 foot square, yet the ponds, Arch, Marble, materials, removal, workmanship, & all the charges of this small building cost att the least £500, which is rather remembered as Caution against too much love of building.⁶⁹

The new banqueting house must have been quite something. It had steps of blue and white Bletchington marble, and Whitelocke loved it. He fenced off an area of about twenty acres around it, and created a rural idyll…..

….in this little Parke, he had Connies⁷⁰, Hares, Pheasants, Partridges, Pigeons, fish ponds, Redde & fallow Deer, & in it was his banqueting house stored with good books, & looking into all parts of it, too much of pleasure to have long continuance, or to have ones heart sett upon it. I could see the game playing around me, & some of them would take meate out of my hand out of the window.

Whitelocke enjoyed entertaining at Fawley Court, much to the chagrin of his old family retainer, William Cooke. William advised him that he needed a wife to manage his domestic affairs, and just such a person was living at the New House in Hambleden with her aunt, the dowager Countess of Sunderland.

….He took account & advice for the management of his private estate. And made use of William Cooke, an old servant & tenant to his father, who spake his mind plainly to his Master telling him that the resort of so much company to him was too chargeable & would in time waste his estate, for oddes would beate any gentleman, he told him likewise that many of his goods were imbeziled and lost for want

---

68 Should have used W J Webb & Son Ltd!
69 The oldest foundations of Fawley Court, under the present building, suggest that Whitelocke's house stood, at least in part, on the site of the present one. No trace has been found of the banquetting house. The higher ground is across the present Henley/Malow road, but the 1842 Tithe Map names field 56 (between the Marlow Road and the river)'Banqueting Field.' Perhaps on the site of Toad Hall?
70 Rabbits.

Appendix 3: Cormorants and Lovebirds

of a woman to looke to them, & wished him to thinke of getting a good wife to help him in household matters, wherin he had no skill, & recommended to him the Countess of Sunderland's Niece Mistress Wiloughby, who lived with her Aunt att Hambleden & was (he said) a comely houswifly maiden.

The young lady in question was twenty-year-old Frances Willoughby (see portrait), daughter of the 3rd Baron Willoughby of Parham.

Initially, Whitelocke affected not to be interested in seeking a second wife, but he soon found an excuse to visit the Countess, assuring himself that he was so far from any thought of wooing that he went along in his old working clothes, his hair unkempt and looking about 50[71]. An unlikely story!

….After his return home[72], he tooke order to clense the great pond or mote at Fawley Court[73], being overgrown with weeds, & unwholesome with the deepe mudde in it, & the water being among springes rising and falling with the Thames, was difficult to be gotten out, butt

for their helpe in it, his people had borrowed an Engine, which the Countesse of Sutherland's miller used bout his waterworks, & the Countess willingly lent it to Whitelocke which stood him in great stead in that work & he thought himself obliged

---

71 He was 29.
72 From a trip to Dorset.
73 Perhaps the inlet of water between the house and the Thames as depicted in this modern image, rather than a moat of which no trace has been found.

> *in civility to waite on the Countesse to give her thankes for it, & he was so farre from any thoughts of wooing, that he went with his haire all overgrown on his face, so that he appeared as one 50 years old, his doublet was of black leather, his breeches of course hair stuffe, in mourning, only his horse was hansome & the French boy waiting on him in good clothes.*

He was talking to the Countess when her niece came into the room, and Whitelocke was smitten....

> *....In this Equipage he waited on the Countesse, & was received by her with all civility and respect, whilest they were discourcing, her Niece Mistress Willoughby came into the roome; her habit was plain but neate, her person was most beautiful and lovely, so that upon the first sight of her, Whitelocke was strangely surprised, & struck with an high affection for her. She herselfe told him afterwards, that when she and the gentlewomen with her, heard that Mr Whitelocke was with her Aunt, she said in drollerye, come lett us goe see the widower, perhappes we may have good of him & thereupon she came into the Roome, which she used not to do when there were strangers.*

He realised that that he had to win over the Countess if he was going to get anywhere with Frances....

> *....Whitelocke minded Mistress Willoughby more than his discourse with the Countesse, yet concealed his wounds[74], only he gave occasion by the offer of his service & attendance upon the Countess, for her to invite him & to tell him what he desired to hear, that he should be welcome to Hambleden. He said nothing to William Cooke, nor to any other, of this rencontre, nor did he presently pursue it.*

He struck on the notion of taking them both cormorant fishing in the hope he may find an opportunity to declare his affection....

---

74 Affection

Appendix 3: Cormorants and Lovebirds

....A short time later, he visited the Lady Sunderland & saw her niece with her & both of them were very civill to him, he waited on them a fishing with his Cormorants, & shewed them excellent sport, with which they were much delighted, & by often visits, being well acquainted in the house, he tooke an opportunity of privacy with the young Lady, & frankly made known his affection & suit to her, & received a modest and generall answear, and no denying from her, which gave him some hopes and incouragement in that buisnes.

The Countess encouraged the courtship....

....Shortly after, with the consent of his Mistress[75], he acquainted her Aunt with his suit & Purpose, & desired her leave, that he might be a suitor & servant to her niece, & to have her Ladyship's favour & assistance therein, & he informed her of his estate, butt enquired nothing touching her Niece's portion. The Countess was not displeased with the motion, butt freely and with liking, gave way to him to be a suitor to her Niece, & he lost no opportunity to make use of that favour butt endeavoured, & not in vain, to settle himself in the affection of his Mistress, & God was pleased exceedingly to blesse them therin.

Things seemed to be going so well that he invited them to Fawley Court....

....The Countess and her Niece, did much delight in fishing, & Whitelocke was good att that sport, & often waited on them with his Cormorants, & with a whery which he had for the pleasure of the River, with a well[76] in it, Anchors, Oares, and sayle, & in this boat, the Countess and hr niece, did him the honour sometimes to be rowed from Mill End to Fawley Court, where they were pleased to accept the entertainment of the place & were delighted in talking with his boy, who did strangely court Mistress Willoughby, as if he had known his father's desires & affection towards her whom the childe called

---

75 This is how he described Frances. She was not his mistress in the modern sense.
76 A tank in which the fish could be preserved alive.

> Lady, & oftentimes such little accidents, testify a providence in a main buisnes as this was to the father.
>
> The Countess was also much delighted with musicke wherein she was skillfull herself, and kept a great Master of musicke in her house, & in this likewise Whitelocke's company was pleasing to her, & she seemed much taken with the musicke in his house wherewith sometimes he entertained her.

Considered a particularly edifying practice, music was praised for its benefits both to the individual, and to society as a whole in the early seventeenth century, and there was a growing demand for music books for domestic use. It seems likely that one of their favourite pieces would have been *My Ladye Nevells Booke*, composed in 1591 by William Byrd. Elizabeth Neville was closely associated with Byrd as a patron, and the book was probably a gift to her. Married to Sir Robert D'Oyley in 1572, she had lived principally at Greenlands, not too far from Harlington, Middlesex, where the Byrd family resided from 1577 to 1594. Lady Neville founded a charity school at Henley and when she died in 1621 she was buried in St Mary's, Henley where a monument commemorates her life. Whitelocke and his father would surely have known her.

The Countess reciprocated Whitelocke's hospitality by inviting him to meals at Hambleden....

> ....By these pleasing means, & by often waiting on her, or rather on her Niece, & seeking to humour her, he gained so much in the Countess's favour, that she often invited him to meales, an unusual favour from her who lived most retiredly, though very nobly, & Whitelocke was not shye to accept these favours, she also honoured him with her presence att his house, & with the presence of his dearest Mistress who was her constant & only Companion.

The time had come for Whitelocke to seek the approval of the senior male members of the family....

> ....He made use of all favours and opportunities (& the Countess saw it) to promote his interest in her Niece's affection, the which he gained

Appendix 3: Cormorants and Lovebirds

prosperously, & to remove obstructions he intreated the Countess & his Mistress to write to Lady Willoughby, sister of the Countess & mother to her Niece, to acquaint her with his suit to her daughter, and to intreat her approbation of it, & to the same effect to write to the Lord Willoughby, & to the Earl Rutland her Uncle, to whom he was a stranger.

Their support was not forthcoming. The Earl of Rutland soon put a stop to any further romantic intentions; his niece (and her inheritance) could not be allowed to fall into the hands of a commoner. Whitelocke was forbidden from visiting the New House....

....By this time, through the Blessing of God, Whitelocke had gained a firme interest in the affection of her whom he best loved, & it fell out happily for him that it was so, there being now sett on foot some attempts and designes to crosse him in it, whereof he had notice from a loving neighbour that the Earl of Rutland, & the Lord Willoughby, had bin att Hambleden, & sought to hinder his happiness, and to brake of the match between him and his Mistress, & that this was endeavoured in his absence in London.

He returned quickly[77] into the Countrye to Hambleden to his deare Mistress who was still the same to him, though the Countenance & humour of her Aunt was much altered. His beard being trimmed, and he better clothed than before was not unpleasing, & now his servants and neighbours tooke notice of his being a suitor to Mistress Willoughby, which some envyed.

From his Mistress chiefly, and from others, he learned that her brother the Lord Willoughby had bin att Hambleden & sent for William Cooke, as William also told him, that her brother & her Uncle the Earle of Rutland were both against her match with Whitelocke & that the Earl had positively written to his Sister not to permit it to proceed, nor to suffer him any more to visit his Niece; the Countess herselfe told Whitelocke in effect as much, & that it was the opinion

---

77 From London

> of the nearest & best of her Niece's friends, that it would not be a convenient match for her with Whitelocke & desired that it might proceed no further.

Whitelocke could not understand why, at this late stage in their relationship, he was being asked to cease all contact with Frances. He protested that he was not after her money….

> ….Whitelocke answeared that he esteemed her Ladyship the nearest & best of her Niece's friends, & next to her Mother, & that he had her consent to the Match, & did much wonder that now it should be endeavoured to be broken off, after so long and hopeful a progresse in it, & nothing propounded on his part for settlement of Estate, butt should be made good, by her Niece's friends, & no contradiction before this by any of them. Butt the Countess replyed, that upon further consideration of the business, it was now their desire and judgement, that this match should not proceed, & she desired Whitelocke to forbeare any further applications to her Niece in that way, & in effect forbid him her house.

He was at pains to emphasise that he had behaved honourably at all times….

> ….He considered that in this business he had used no indirect or unlawful means, that there was no dishonour or dishonest ends in it, that he had taken order for her mother, brother & Uncle to be acquainted with it, that her Mother had not contradicted it, that her brother was a young lord who had not the disposing of his Sister, that her Uncle had his Niece's portion in his hands, & occasions for the use of it, that her Aunt had approved it, & now after it had gone so farre & their affections settled, to commaund it as their Lordship's pleasure to be broken off, could not well be digested by Whitelocke nor would his affections submit to it, which were faithful and engaged, & therefore he resolved, notwithstanding his great opposers, to endeavour to accomplish his just and honest ends, & to make himself happy by it.

Appendix 3: Cormorants and Lovebirds

Whitelocke would not be put off. He sent notes to Frances hidden within the produce that William Cooke's wife took to the Countess at the New House....

> ....*This was a severe sentence, & put Whitelocke into great perplexity & trouble & now his personal attendance being prohibited, he made his addresses to his Mistress by letters in a private way, by means of William Cooke's wife, who formerly used to bring little Countrey presents to her, & now began again that trade, & in the bottom of her basket had usually a letter to his Mistress from Whitelocke & carried back her answear to him, also he had a good friend in the house, an antient gentlewoman, kinswoman of the Countess & her Niece, who by complements and presents he had won to his party, & she furthered his suit with his Mistress: and sometimes delivered his letters.*

Together they planned an elopement. On November 9, Frances left the New House ostensibly to go for a walk with a maidservant and two elderly gentlemen of the household, but in fact to jump into Whitelocke's coach, get married secretly in his private chapel at Fawley Court, and escape with him to London for a honeymoon at the Ship Inn in Fleet Street....

> ....*His Mistress was alike engaged, & distasted with the proceedings of her friends & they layd & contrived their designes of effecting their honest & just intentions, & God was pleased to blesse them in it. He went att Michaelmas terme to London, whither the antient gentlewoman was comes from Hambleden, & by her, Whitelocke had opportunity without suspitions to send to his Mistress & to contrive their meeting, & about Allhollantide[78], by appointment, Whitelocke & the antient gentlewoman came late over night to Fawley Court, & the next morning early, he and 6 gentlemen his trusty friends whom he brought down with him went in the Coach neere to the place where the appointment was to meet with Mistress Willoughby, being a field not far from Hambleden house, whither she used often*

---

78   A variant of All Hallowstide, a period which begins on 31 October.

to walke to take the aier[79]. By the way he left his friends, & att the place happily he met this Mistress with a maide & 2 of her Aunt's gentlemen waiting on her.

After salutations, Whitelocke told his Mistress that the weather was cold and bad for her to walke, & intreated her to make use of his Coach, she civilly accepted, butt when he was leading her to it, the gentlemen suspecting somewhat began to bustle & came up to him to take her from him, he layd his hand on his sword[80] & told them it would not be easy to take his Mistress out of his hand, that he should first part with his life, that they intended nothing butt was lawful & honourable & he desired them to acquaint their Lady therewith, & that they hoped ere long to waite on her gain, & nothing could prevent their just and honest designes, & for the gentlemen, if they loved their lives, he prayed them to be quiet & to present his humble service to their Lady.

They finding it in vain to struggle any further, Whitelocke brought away his mistress in his Coach, tooke up his friends where he had left them, & came away not slowly to Fawley Court carrying this rich treasure with him, there her kinswoman was to attend upon her. He caused his gates to be shut, & they went presently into the Chappell, where the Parson of Fawley[81], being ready, they were marryed, & after a short breakfast they took Coach & drove apace to London to hansom lodgings near the Temple, whither divers of their friends came to them, and rejoyced with them.

Within a short time, they were welcomed back to Hambleden….

….They went to Fawley Court before Christmas where their neighbours & friends & tenants were wellcome to them, some of her

---

79 Probably Whitelocke left the carriage in Dairy Lane (formerly Mill End Lane) and Frances came along 'Lady's Walk', the footpath through or just below Great Wood which would have afforded some privacy.
80 Interesting that he should wear a sword for his elopement!
81 Rev William Kitson.

Appendix 3: Cormorants and Lovebirds

relations did them the favour to visit them, & the Countess of Sunderland admitted them to her house with all respect.

It truly was a love match, for when he returned to Fawley Court from attending the Oxford assizes, he recorded....

....After this first journey which he had bin from his wife, att his coming home, she mett him leaping for joy at his safe return, as she did att all times after, & they had the great blessing of the height of those joys & comforts which true love affordes in Conjugall society, and what God was pleased to deny in the former[82], his goodness did fully supply in this time with advantage.[83]

The marriage lasted for fourteen and a half years, during which time they had nine children.

---

82 His first wife had been very neurotic, and their sex life had been a disaster. They did, however, manage one son.
83 Whitelocke's candour about his love life reveals him as a passionate man, free from the prudery which was to afflict later Puritans.